THE PREORDAINED COSMOS

HILLAR

outskirtspress
DENVER, COLORADO

Outskirts Press, Inc.
http://www.outskirtspress.com

ISBN: 978-1-4787-7873-8

Outskirts Press and the "OP" logo are trademarks belonging to Outskirts Press, Inc.

PRINTED IN THE UNITED STATES OF AMERICA

Contents

1

Introduction

The purpose of this book is to induce interest in the mysterious cosmos and to report what the scientists have discovered about the universe, including the miracle of life. Whether you are a layman or an expert, you will learn about past discoveries, future research and theories based on the present knowledge. It is presented without formulas and mathematical equations, except the renowned Einstein's $E=mc^2$ equation. Whenever a scientific term or word appears in this book, it is usually accompanied with an explanation of the meaning of it. If no source or author is disclosed on any scientific discovery or research report in the narrative of this book, it is a general knowledge available on the internet to everybody. Cosmologists technique of acquiring information by observation and experimentation is called "Scientific method". Also, knowledge acquired by senses is included in the "scientific method", except revelations, theology, and spirituality. This method was disputed by Einstein, who declared " Science without a religion is lame and religion without a science is blind". The purpose of acquiring empirical evidence is to discover whether the conjectures and hypothesis are falsifiable. If they are unfalsifiable, cosmologists call them unscientific and classify them as pseudoscience. To be classified as a scientific method, it requires the experiments to be reproducible and verifiable by others. By using exactly the same methods and equipment for the experiment, the results would be always the same. It will not determine whether it is falsifiable or unfalsifiable. The irony is that many "scientific theories" are just falsifiable hypothesis based on assumptions, hidden variables, probabilities or the formula has virtual and fictional ingredient. The information acquired by this method is not "evidence" and any theory based on it is not only falsifiable, it is an uncertain conjecture. The uncertainty necessitates either continuous revisions of the postulated "scientific" theories or completely discarding the old conjectures and hypothesis. Under the uncertainty principle, it is impossible to know the position and the momentum simultaneously, or to establish maxims. All physical, religious, mythological and metaphysical historical cosmologies are based on assumptions or beliefs. None of them can be tested or scientifically proven . The complexity of life and most of the inexplicable phenomena of the cosmos are beyond our present day physics and remain as mysteries, summarized in the COMPENDIUM.

2 | Miracle of Life

The estimated number of stars in the observable universe is over hundred billion trillion (100,000,000,00 0,000,000,000,000 +). Astronomer believe that most stars have exoplanetary systems with incalculable number of planets. Thus the odds for other intelligent life in the universe should be assured. To verify any other life in the universe, we must discover planets with conditions suitable for life as we know it. There are over 200 critical requirements and conditions for carbon base life we enjoy on earth. Even if one condition is off more than a fraction of a percentage, intelligent life is not possible. The odds are astronomically high for finding another planet in the universe, which meets all the same conditions as on earth. To this date astronomers have not discovered any other intelligent life in the outer space. Individual reports of supernatural encounters with aliens, angles and other mysterious beings are personal spiritual experiences. Also, the sightings of UFO's and other unexplained occurrences provide no evidence for extraterrestrial life. Even if there is other intelligent life in the universe, the question is: "How it got there?"

The origin of life on earth, about 3.83 billion years ago, and the complexity of it is still a mystery. To claim that life originated in primordial soup, it must contain 1. Proteins, 2. Nucleic acids (DNA &RNA). 3 Polysaccharides and 4. Lipids, made from carbon based molecules. Since all four nucleotide building blocks degrade in 158-195° F temperature, the beginning of life would have to be virtually instantaneous in primordial temperatures on earth. Even when the earth cooled, the two biochemical features for life are: 1. Self-replication (its own reproduction) and 2. Metabolism (chemical pathways for complex web of molecules). The problem is that DNA (deoxyribonucleic acid) is not self-replicating molecule and without the DNA the cell cannot produce proteins. Without a source for proteins, there is no carbon-based life possible. Francis Crick and James Watson discovered that DNA was the carrier of specific genetic information in the form of chemicals represented by letters A, C,

T and G. The sequence of these chemicals provided the instructions for assembling complex protein molecules for all parts of human bodies, including the intricate eyes and the incomparable human brain. At the latest count human bodies contain 37.2 trillion cells using 20 different amino-acids to form biomolecules. Each human cell has definite biochemical information system and codes forming an intricate molecular machine made up from over 100 trillion atoms. It is

more complicated than any machine built by a man. The structures of cells called Mitochondria with 16,500 nucleotides is inherited only through mother. There are over 3 billion nucleotide positions in the human genome containing over 20,500 genes. Human genes are composed of DNA, a molecule in the strand of double helix combined into 23 pairs or a total of 46 chromosomes. The last pair is either the X or male chromosomes and Y or female sex chromosomes. Deleterious gene mutations, caused by radiation from outer space and other damaging sources on earth, have lead to a range of sex-related disorders. The mutations cause 600 to 6300 nucleotide substitutions per person per generation. Applying average of 1200 mutations to every nucleotide positions in the human genome the accumulated effect has been and will continue to cause permanent genetic damage. The original lifespan of humans used to be up thousand years. The bombardment of earth from super novae, black holes gamma rays and other radiation has accelerated the human DNA mutations. The present life expectancy is less than 120 years and the accumulated mutation damage to human genome is causing serious problems for a long term survival. More and more human beings are having questions about their sexual orientation. The increase in homosexuality, transsexual and other abnormal behavior is the direct result of damaged DNA. The sex of the baby is determined by the male sperm with either X or Y chromosome. Male Y chromosome SRY (Sex-determining Region Y) protein is responsible for sex determination of male organs and preventing development of female reproductive structures. After the X chromosome female egg is fertilized with a male X or Y chromosome, the female X chromosome is inactivated. If the female X chromosome is still active, it can generate XX and YX chromosomes, or mutate to XXX and other combination of chromosomes. The information sequence found in DNA and in other biomolecules are similar to the computer software - the undisputed product of conscious intelligence. Even Dawkins (The author of "The God Delusion") reluctantly agreed "The machine code of genes is uncannily computer-like".

Scientists at Northwestern University in Chicago discovered a stunning bright light signaling the moment of conception. When the male sperm entered the female egg a surge of calcium triggered the release of zinc sparks from the fertilized egg. This is a definite sign for the beginning of spiritual life in the physical life of a baby. Human life, whether it starts in or outside the female body, is a new creation of life. When a female egg is retrieved from ovaries and fertilized by sperm in the lab, it is creating life "In vitro fertilization". By creating new life, geneticists are parturient in the conception and also the destroyers of unwanted life. Any time life is created and then killed, whether in the lab or in uterus by intrauterine device (IUD) by stopping the fertilized egg implanting or growing in the wall of the uterus, is abortion. Male sperms killed by IUD before fertilization, are not killing life. Since males produce over 525 billion sperms during their lifetime, only very few are the source for new life.

Deleterious mutations and micro evolution are part of entropy and not new creations. At the end of every year we call the next year a "New Year". This is a misnomer! The fact is, universe and everything in it is one year older. The Second Thermodynamics law declares that all visible and invisible matter in the universe is subject to unstoppable decaying or aging, or entropy. The actual meaning of entropy is "Turning in on itself". The only way to avoid entropy is either to stop time or revert universe back to 0° degrees (-459.67°F or -273.15°C). Since the universe is +2.735° kelvin or degrees above the absolute 0, the entropy remains unabated. There is no "Macro" evolution or the creation of "new" species, only micro evolution altering the existing species. The cells of organic life convey all the past effects of entropy in any new creation. Entropy continues to decay all matter to an ultimate state of uniformity. Everything gets older and older and no "new" matter is added to the universe. Or is it? God promised a new earth and a new heaven in Rev 21:1-5. All you have to do is accept Jesus and He will make all things new again and put an end to entropy.

3

Inconceivable Existence

People accept their existence and life on the surface of the earth as a preordained event. They know that the earth rotates once every 24 hours, or once a day. The surface speed of earth is 1,670 km/hr at the equator and gradually decreases to zero at the poles of earth. Time is measured with 24 hour clocks regardless of the location of the observer on the earth surface. Because the 7918 mile diameter earth's rotation is gradually slowing, our 24 hour clocks have been changed from Greenwich Mean Time (GMT) to Coordinated Universal Time (UTC). The UTC is a combination of the International Atomic Time (TAI) with Universal Time (UT1) measure of the actual length of day on earth. The movement of earth, in addition to the rotation speed, is governed by the 901,242 km/hr speed around the sun, the solar system's 828,000 km/hr rotation speed within the Milky Way galaxy and the postulated 267,480 km/hr expansion of the entire observable universe. However, this trillion plus km/hr combined velocity of earth's rotation, orbital speed around the sun, the Milky Way rotational speed and the expansion of the universe, cause no sense of motion to the people on the surface of the earth. Velocity is a relative term depending where the observer is. As an example: Let's assume a spaceship in earth's orbit is moving 100 feet per second and you drop an article 10 feet from the ceiling of the spaceship and it lands on the floor in one second. To the space traveler the velocity of the article was 10 feet per second, however if the observer was on earth the velocity of the article was approx. 100.5 feet per second. The earth's 24 hour time is also impacted by the 9.807 m/s² gravity (meters per second squared) velocity or 32.174 foot acceleration of all the objects on earth. In the theory of relativity time dilation is the result of velocity and gravity. The1908 essay by Minkowsi, Einstein's teacher, was the first to disclosed the space-time continuum theory proving that velocity effects time and all motion is relative to the point of reference at any time. Einstein only added the curvature of the space-time (gravity) in the General Relativity theory. Time was added as the fourth dimension to the length, width and height in the space-time theory. To reconcile gravity with quantum mechanic, Edward Witten combined in 1995 supersymmetry and general relativity and added six additional strings, expanding it to 10 string dimensional universe. The 10 dimensional string theory contradicted the Big Bang (BB) theory and cosmologists added another dimension, making it total of 11 dimensions. The 11-th dimension in the string theory solved the mathematical problem with the BB theory by incorporating an infinite number of parallel universes and connecting all the matter in one structure with calculated dimension of one trillionth of a centimeter. Cosmologists named it the "Membrane-theory" or simply the "M-theory". Since the 11 dimensional universe is only a conjecture, Witten named it "Magical", or "Mythical", or Mystery" or "Mad" theory.

In the1895 science fiction novel "The Time Machine" H. G Wells proposed travel into the future and back to the present. Although higher velocity slows time and affects aging, but no matter, energy or information can travel faster than the speed of light. The Einstein-Rosen bridges imply hypothetical wormholes as the possible shortcuts between two separate points in space. Time dilation is a phenomena in relativistic physics when:

1. Length contracts

2. Relativistic mass varies with the velocity of the observer

3. Universal speed limit

4. Relativity of simultaneity

In special relativity the cause for slowing time is motion, and in general relativity the cause is gravity. Lorentz Contraction theory also proposes the shrinking of length in the special relativity theory. The results of hypothetical travel at the speed of light (1,079,252,800 km/hr)1. Time stops 2. Mass has only two dimensions, like a picture with infinite amount of energy. Einstein's equations also postulate that "On the fundamental level time does not exist at all and in a "frozen" universe there is no time, only space. Some astrophysicists believe that we live in an essentially atemporal (unaffected by time) world. The hypotheticl extra dimension of time by Itzhak Bars and Michio Kaku by combining everything into one theory, is not testable. The notion that we could travel from one dimension to another dimension or into a parallel universe in the 11 dimensional universe is only possible in science fiction. The hypothesis of multi-verses or an infinite number of parallel universes formed as countless soap bubbles in the 11-th dimension, are only a mathematical fallacy. Until scientifically proven, all these postulations are nothing more than a fantasy.

The presently endorsed BB birth of the universe and the beginning of time includes too many unknown and untestable hypothesis. It completely ignores the cause, the source and the amount of energy in the visible and invisible cosmos. The start of time 13.85 billion of years ago with BB is not a rational theory. Cosmos time is and always has been ETERNAL! No beginning and no end. It is the only realistic conclusion.

4

The Mysterious Universe

All through the ages people have marveled about the mysteries of the universe. The scientific discoveries of the universe leave us full of awe and wonder. This chapter will explain in layman's terms the many known and unknown aspects of cosmos.

The present estimated diameter of the observable universe is 93 billion light years. One light-year, or the distance light travels in one year, is 5,879 billion miles or 0.3066 Parsecs. Parsecs are based on the average distance of earth from the sun and one parsec is 3.26 light years or 19.2 trillion miles. The actual speed of the light is 186,282 mp/s! According to the latest research, the observable universe is 13.82 billion light years old. Applying the value of the 93 billion light year diameter of the universe to the age of the universe, the size of the universe is 6.73 (93/13.82) times larger than it is possible with the speed of light expansion and at least 3.37 times larger, if earth is in the center of the universe and universe has 46.5 billion light-year radius. However, faster than the speed of light expansion of the universe or "Inflation" violates the present day physics of "Nothing with mass can travel faster than the speed of light". Based on this maxim, either the 13.82 billion light year age of the universe, as reported by the latest Planck research, or the 93 billion light year diameter universe is wrong, or the "Speed of light squared" in the $E=mc^2$ equation is only a mathematical hypothesis. The conclusion is: Either the universe without inflation is at least 46.5 light years old, or the diameter of the observable universe is not more than 27.64 (13.82x2) billion light years, depending on the location of earth relative to the source of BB.

The controversial expansion of the universe has many theories. In 1929 Edwin Hubble (11/20/1889 - 9/28/1953) discovered the distance to a given galaxy is proportional to the recessional velocity measured as the Doppler "red shift". This was later accepted as the Hubble's Law with Hubble's constant. The extended Hubble's model, now called the Lambada-CDM (Cold Dark Matter) Model of cosmological constants in a quantum vacuum includes six fixed parameters, six independent parameters and ten calculated values, with 68% confidence limits for dark energy. The present consensus by the cosmologists is "The observed red shift of all the distant galaxies indicates that the universe is expanding". The expansion can occur in the open, flat or close universe. The open universe is a continually expanding and never stopping infinite universe. The flat universe is expanding and eventually stopping at some time in the future. The closed universe is slowing to a stop and then collapsing into a super-massive black hole, called Big Rip, Big Bounce, Big Freeze or Big Crunch. According to the present theory, our universe is almost flat. In a flat expanding universe all the galaxies can move away from earth only if the earth is in the center of the universe. The red shift observation of all the spreading galaxies is only possible in an orderly isotropic universe. There are many other theories about the red shift of galaxies, but most cosmologists accept the expansion phenomena without any explanation. The dark flow, or all the galaxies moving in one direction, has been discarded after the 2013 Planck spacecraft observation showing no dark flow of the universe. The question remains "What causes the red shift of all the distant galaxies?" In 1842 Christian Doppler discovered that the increased wave length of the electromagnetic radiation was caused by the stretching or scattering of light. In 1929 Zwincky predicted the Quantum Electromagnetic (QED) induced red shift. The cosmological red shift is the result of the lower energy of photons visible on earth. Marmet, a senior researcher at Herzbeg Institute of Astrophysics of the National research Council of Canada, in his 1993 book entitled "Absurdities in Modern Physics" corrected the expansion of the universe with QED red shift and totally discredited the BB and General Relativity theories of it. In the present theories of Higgs field releasing photons when particles obtain mass, the presence of astrophysical plasma and the dark energy or vacuum energy being everywhere in the universe, would be the cause for faster radiation of the red shift from distant galaxies than the postulate from the CMBR observation for the expanding the universe.

Universe contains gravitationally bound galaxy filaments of supercluster complexes, with orderly designs of galaxy walls, galaxy sheets, large quasar groups and Lyman-alpha blobs (LAB), consisting of one-electron ions in the spectral line of hydrogen. The largest structure in the universe is the 2013 discovery of the long Hercules-Corona Borealis Great Wall, measuring over 3 Gpe (Megaparsecs) or 10 billion light years. One megaparsec is one million parsecs and one parsec is 3.26 billion light years or 19 trillion miles. This discovery totally invalidates the cosmological principle of isotropic universe. The late Carl Sagan always postulated that there are "Billions and billions of stars in the universe and it was all a waste of space". He had no idea about the intricate design of the universe and the critical amount of matter required for our life on this earth. In the anisotropic universe nothing is wasted or dispersed accidentally. The latest estimate of over 225 billion galaxies in the observable universe are in perfect formations.

In addition to the visible radiation of light, the universe is filled with electromagnetic radiations from 40 Extremely low frequency to tremendously high frequency Radio waves, followed by spectrum of Microwave, Infrared, Ultraviolet, X- rays and finally the gamma rays. According to the present theory, all radiation is transmitted by waves and includes observable photon energy with wavelength, amplitude, velocity and frequency. The waves are disturbances in material or medium when one part influences the next. The question is: How can waves transmit radiation in an empty space or in a vacuum without any medium? Either the radiation is NOT transmitted by waves or the empty space is not really "empty" and some other unknown "medium" transmits the radiation. "Empty space" or vacuum can transmit CMBT (Cosmic Background microwave Radiation), light (Electromagnetic radiation), gravitational waves, antinutrinos, Gamma rays, X-rays, ultraviolet, infrared an radio waves and has electric and magnetic components? One of the postulates of transmission is "Vacuum energy of space" with virtual pairs of subatomic particles. For more details see THE SECETS OF COSMOS article.

The current scientific theory of "Wave-particle duality" also applies to atoms and molecules as the medium containing mass. The latest theory is: The sunlight has no mass or electric charge and the Electromagnetic force is carried by "virtual" photons and their anti-photons. Radiation is a form of energy and energy equals the velocity of the mass at the speed of light squared $(mc^2=E)$. The question is: What is actually transmitted when the source of the radiation does not lose any mass? In the Quantum Field Theory (QFT) the Quantum Mechanics and the Special Relativity are reconciled with the hypothesis that the elementary particles are either point-like objects of zero intrinsic size or quasi particles. If the hypothetical Tachyon particles with imaginary mass could travel faster than the speed of light, they would violate the causality clause, which is not possible under the present physics. Science has not been able to explain how particles can obtain mass in the Higgs field or how the mass is transmitted in the vacuum. It remains an unsolved mystery.

There are many other theories of parallel universe or multiverses. Science fiction has proposed alternative universes in other dimensions, like the Lorentzian transferable wormholes from one universe to another. Or the unproven postulation of Einstein-Rosen bridge of wormhole travel in spacetime between vacuum solutions, where there are no gravitational sources or mass. Time travel to the future and into the past have fascinated the young and the curious at heart. Comic books, television, video games on fantasy lands and future worlds have been and are still very popular. It was back in 1895 when H. G. Wells books The Time Machine, The Wonderful Visit, Men Like Gods and fourth dimension Time Traveler, were the hits of a paranormal adventure. Even the Wizard of OZ lived in a land of OZ.

5

Realistic Theory of Galaxies

1. Standard Model vs. Realistic Theory

There are about 200 billion galaxies in the universe. The diameters of the galaxies vary from 1,000 to 100,000 parsecs, or from 3,260 to 326,000 light years. One light year is about 9 trillion kilometers. Recent discovery of supermassive black holes in the centers of most galaxies has posed many questions and produced several hypothesis. In the Standard Model (SM) theory the black holes are the result of the supermassive stars supernovae. The estimated size of the supermassive black hole in the center of the Milky Way galaxy is at least four million times more massive than our sun. This is based on the observation of S2 star orbit around the location of Sagittarius A in the center of Milky

Way. Black holes with one solar mass would have about three kilometer radius, or two hundred million times smaller radius than our sun Although most black holes are not visible, their existence can be observed by the effect they have on the surrounding space. About 10% of galaxies have luminous type I or type II Seyfert radioactive nucleus. Seyfert type I galaxies are in active hypernovae and the black holes have a very bright nucleus radiating x-rays and gamma rays. When the hypernova ends the luminosity of type II galaxy nucleus dims leaving a black hole in the center of galaxy. Cosmologists claim that nothing can escape from the black hole, whether it is matter, light or time. This gravitational force is condensed into infinite density called "singularity". However, there is no proof for the hypothetical gravitational singularity in the centers of black holes. The one-dimensional single point singularity, containing huge mss with infinite density, gravity and infinitely curved space-time is beyond the laws of the present physics. Scientists have no rational concept of infinity and the black holes remain a mystery. Magnetars and microquasars or mini quasars, formed after the primordial hyper-giant stars hyper-novae, are thought to be the stellar black holes in a binary star system, consisting of a normal star and a compact object emitting x-rays and gamma rays. Another possibility for the compact objects are pulsars emitting electromagnetic radiation (EM) of radio waves, infrared light, microwaves, visible light, ultraviolet radiation, x-rays and gamma rays.

The supermassive black hole in the center of the Milky Way is the direct result of a hyper-novae of the primordial hyper-giant star. So are the supermassive black holes in the center of most galaxies in the universe. The latest NASA's Chandra Observatory x-ray observation of NGC 5195 galaxy showed a supermassive black hole expelling matter outward into the surrounding space. According to SM theory, matter passing the "Event horizon" or the edge of the black hole, will be drawn into the black hole. The reality is, black holes do not suck matter in, they expel the outer shell of the star during the hyper-novae. Astrophysicists have never observed an event horizon and only postulate the "feeding" black holes. Quasars or Active Galatic Nuclei

(AGN) surrounding the center of young galaxies, emitting electromagnetic energy, radio waves and light, also indicate the location of emerging black holes.

Galaxies are created when electroweak force fuses neutrons to hydrogen protons forming the nuclei of deuterium atoms, or the H-1 hydrogen isotope. The gravity causes the deuterium to burn and as the fusion process continues more protons are added to the nuclei of atoms forming the next element Helium He-2 with two protons, then Lithium Li-3 with three protons. When the Iron Fe-26 element with 26 protons is reached, it is the critical stage before the hyper-novae. The larger the star the quicker it burns and the deuterium in the super giant stars are depleted in a few million years. In the last stages Iron Fe-26, Cobalt Co-27 and Nickel Ni-28 generate enormous amount of magnetic fields and the stars expand into type 'O' super-giant red stars up to thousands of times larger than the original stars. In the final stage, called Wolf-Rayet, the stars explode in hyper-nova, spreading visible matter with magnetic fields into the surrounding space to form the galaxy.

Asassn-15lh supernova about 3.8 billion years from earth, was 50 times more luminous than Milky Way galaxy, when Wolf-Rayet star exploded after losing the outer layer of hydrogen and then fusing helium and heavier elements. This was the birth of primordial galaxies and now the continuing source for planets, nebulae, interstellar media and second generation stars.

2. Visible and Dark Matter

In the present theory universe contains of 4.9% visible matter, 26.8% dark matter and 68.3% dark energy. The visible matter in the universe is comprised of 75% of hydrogen, 23% of helium, 1% of oxygen and 1% of nitrogen, neon, carbon and other heavier elements. The latest theory is: Visible matter obtained mass in Higgs Field from the Higgs bosons or God's particles.

The first hydrogen atoms consisted of subatomic elementary particles called quarks and leptons. Combined with the charged leptons and the W &Z bosons, or weak interaction force, they were the basic building blocks of matter. Electrons are charged leptons and neutrinos are neutral leptons. All atoms have one negatively charged electron acting as a particle or a wave. Electrons are the source for gravity, electromagnetic force, weak interaction, electricity, magnetism and thermal conductivity. The four bosons, or force carriers in SM, are one of two fundamental classes of particles, the other is fermions. Electrons, protons and neutrons are fermions. The first isotope of hydrogen H-1, called protium, from the Greek word proton or "first", is a subatomic particle composed of three quarks. The quarks are held together by kinetic energy and gluon fields, or the strong force. Quarks, anti-quarks and gluons, or gauge bosons, are elementary particles called hadrons. First isotope of hydrogen atom, called protium, has one proton in the nucleus. Deuterium, or the "second" isotope of hydrogen, has a proton plus a neutron. Atoms with additional protons in the nucleus are the heavier elements and the atomic number of the element is based on the number of protons in the nucleus of the atom.

There has been no "Big Bang" beginning for the universe or cosmic inflation. Read THE BIG BANG CONTROVERSY article. The hypothesis of Big Bang fails to identify the source and the amount of the unified or "fundamental" force for the birth of the universe. Also, inflation, or faster than the speed of light expansion of the universe is impossible under the present physical laws. From the beginning of time, Higgs Field or God's force/energy was and still is everywhere in the universe. This unified force/ energy of gravity, weak interaction with electromagnetic force and nuclear or strong force was contained in all the subatomic particles. This energy/force converted these subatomic particles into visible mass of proton particles as the first element of hydrogen and then added neutrons for the hydrogen isotope deuterium. The force/ energy compressed the deuterium particles into the primordial hyper-giant stars establishing the centers for every galaxy in the universe. The fusion process of these hyper-giant hydrogen stars generated other heavier elements for the second generation stars, planets, interstellar media and the magnetic fields. After the deuterium fuel in the stars was depleted the hype-novae distributed the visible matter and the magnetic fields to form each galaxy.

Under he present SM theory dark matter and

Higgs field are everywhere in the universe. After scientists at LHC discovered the predicted Higgs particle (boson) decay in the July 4, 2012 experiment, they also postulated the existence of the Higgs field. In the hypothetical Higgs field the Higgs bosons would provide mass to all other particles for the visible universe. This hypothesis contradicts the BB epochs, based on the single unified or "fundamental" force. It is surmising that scientists, after searching for a theory of everything (TOE) they finally deiced on a single force for the cause of the Big Bang and the birth of the universe. Whether the subatomic particles obtained mass in the Higgs field or from the primordial plasma epochs, there was not enough force/gravity from the visible matter to maintain the steady shape of the galaxies. They added fictitious "dark" matter to compensate for the lack of total force/gravity in order to keep the stars in permanent galaxy formation. The word "matter" is absolutely misleading. Actually it was the force/gravity and not "dark" matter what was required. According to this theory each galaxy must have the exact amount of total force/energy to counter the centrifugal force of the rotating galaxy or they will fly apart. Secondly, the galaxies must have "dark" matter in addition to the visible matter to maintain the formation or collapse into a super-massive black hole in the center of galaxies. The black holes are beyond the laws of Einstein's Field Equations (EFE) in the General Relativity and in Quantum Mechanics. In the present Standard Model cosmology, called Lambda-CDM Model, the assumption is that quantum vacuum is the cosmological constant for the "dark" matter. But there are no known methods to validate the actual cosmological constant. Unless this crucial problem in cosmology is solved, this theory is only a postulate or hypothesis based on assumption. True, the total amount of gravity in the galaxies must be balanced, but how it is balanced remains an unsolved mystery. Either the necessary amount of total gravity required to balance the galaxies are included in every subatomic particle's inherent "information" or the amounts of the hypothetical dark matter and the visible matter are controlled by outside source. There is no proof for the existence of "dark" matter or even any hypothesis how the gravitational balance of the galaxy is achieved. Also, there are no credible theories how the subatomic particles obtained the information or the necessary amount of gravity to accurately balance the galaxies, or what controls the balance. There must be permanent gravitational fields to keep the galaxies from flying apart and the magnetic fields to maintain the shape of the galaxy. Although there are some moving clusters of newborn stars within the galaxy, which were formed after the hyper-nova of the primordial hyper-giant star, the stars and planets as a whole, rotate in unison with the primordial black hole. To believe that the gravity of all the stars in the galaxy is accidentally balanced with the conjectural dark matter or by a chance, is fallacious. It is the force/gravity of the primordial black holes in the center of every galaxy and the magnetic fields that keep the galaxies in formation and not the dark matter.

3. Summary

Most galaxies rotate around primordial super-massive "Black Holes". The black holes are remnants of the hyper-novae of the primordial hyper-giant stars in the center of galaxies. The force/gravity of these primordial black holes keep the stars, planets, nebulae and other interstellar media from flying into space and the magnetic fields keep them from falling back into the black holes. It is this fictitious gravitational field of the primordial back holes in the center of the galaxies and the magnetic fields coiled around in spiral patterns that keep the visible matter of galaxies in formation and not the mysterious dark matter. Although cosmologists have no concept of the origin or the existence of the dark matter, they continue to use this supposition as a fact in the structure of galaxies. They accept the existence of gravity, nuclear force or strong force and electromagnetism/weak interaction force, but they do not disclose the source of them. The latest claim that the Big Bang started from these four unified forces, or the "fundamental" force, is an unproven postulate. The vacuum or dark energy filled the universe from the beginning of time and is still everywhere in the universe. This is the source for the expansion and the maintenance of our universe. For further details see THE SECRETS OF COSMOS article. The claim that the visible matter in the universe was produced in the hypothetical "Higgs field", where all the subatomic particles obtained mass, is impossible under our present physics. In Einstein's equation of $E=mc^2$ the mass is multiplied by "c^2" or the "Speed of light squared". But there is nothing faster than the speed of light under the present physics. When eliminating the "c^2" or velocity from the $m=E/c^2$ equation, the result is $m=E$. Therefore all mass is energy. Cosmologists can measure the magnetic and gravity fields in the galaxies without knowing the cause or the origin of them. Although there is no proof for the hypothetical "Higgs field" or any of the Quantum Field Theories (QFT), cosmologist accept any theory, regardless how impossible it is, as long as it is not God's creation. Scientists agree that these are the most difficult theories in modern physics, but there is absolutely no possible way to prove them. The truth is: Mass, or the elements in the hydrogen stars and the inherent force/gravity in atoms, which formed the primordial hyper-giant stars, could not happen out of nothing, without a cause. The only possible answer "MASS AND ALL THE FORCE FIELDS WERE CREATED BY GOD"!

6

Incalculable Energy

The visible energy in the universe is mass in the form of matter. According to SM all matter, including living plants, animals and humans are comprised of elementary particles or quarks. If so, it is impossible to comprehend the amount of energy in the visible universe. There are over hundred billion trillion stars with planets, interstellar and intergalatic media. One gram of mass or .035 ounces, or 1.43 penny weight (pwt) is equivalent to either: a) 25million kilowatt hours, b) 21.5 kilotons of TNT, c) 85.2 billion BTU's, d) 568,000 US gallons of gasoline and e) 89.9 terajoules. NOTE: One terajoule is one trillion joules of energy, or work or heat in the International system of units. In addition to visible matter there is invisible energy comprising of gravity, nuclear or strong force, electroweak force, dark energy, and the Higgs, electric, magnetic, etc fields. The present hypothesis is that the source for the inconceivable amount of energy in the cosmos was generated by BB and then distributed by cosmic inflation to everywhere in the universe. However, this hypothesis violates our present physics and there is no proof for this postulate. In Einstein's equation $E= mc^2$ the "Speed of light squared" and the inflation or "Faster than the speed of light" contradict the maxim "Nothing with mass moves faster than the speed of light". Cosmologists never disclose what was the cause for faster than the speed of light or the inflation.

In the SM theory Gravity was separated from the Fundamental force in the Quark epoch of the BB. Although gravity is the "weakest" force on earth, it is also the most mysterious force of the singularity in the Black hole. The gravitational history started with Galileo Galilei over 400 years ago. Sir Isaac Newton published his theory of gravitation in 1687. His equation for the gravitational force F was "Between two bodies directly proportional to the product of their mass and inversely proportional to the square of their distances, times the gravitational constant G". The uncertainty of the original empirical physical constant G value has been revised by "Atom interferometry" and now superseded by a more precise G value with the 2015 study of "Periodic variations". Quantum gravity research and the replication value of the gravitational constant remain a mystery.

In Einstein's General theory of relativity the gravity is "The curvature of spacetime" caused by uneven distribution of mass/energy. Accordingly, all mass in the universe is governed by gravity, regardless how far apart they are. In the spacetime gravitational time dilation theory the stronger the gravitation the slower the time lapses. The effects from the Einstein's Special relativity theory are: 1. Slowing time 2. Shrinking lengths and 3. Increasing mass/energy. At the speed of light this theory concludes: "Time stops and the two dimensional mass with no length has infinite amount of energy". In the Higgs field theory all the subatomic particles obtain mass without imparting or losing any mass/energy. The theory does not explain how the Higgs field could be everywhere in the universe, where the incredible amount of energy came from and how can mass be imparted without losing any energy. Energy can neither be created nor destroyed under the "Law of conservation of energy", only transformed from one form to another. Visible matter has intrinsic or rest mass/energy. It can be converted to equivalent amounts of kinetic energy, potential energy and electromagnetic energy. Energy can be transmitted by mechanical waves like sound and by wave of vibrations from particle to particle. The electromagnetic waves transmit light and radio waves, microwaves, infrared and ultraviolet radiation, x and gamma rays. In all cases the total mass and total energy remains unchanged. To conform with the law of conservation of energy, Wolfgang Pauli predicted the existence of an uncharged invisible particle. Fermi called it "neutrino", emitted along with an electron during beta-decay. It was Pauli who in 1925 proposed his "Exclusion principle" of "Two identical fermions cannot occupy the same quantum state simultaneously". In 1933 Enrico Fermi (1901-1954) described the beta-decay emission not only as a emission of an electron from the nucleus in atomic orbital, but also the emission of an antineutrino, as the missing part of the total energy. Fermi has been called "The architect of the nuclear age and the designer of the atomic bomb". His theoretical and experimental discoveries in statistical nuclear and particle physics were major contributions to the quantum theory. He created the first "Chicago Pile-1" nuclear reactor. Nuclear energy can be produced by fission, fusion and decay. Fission energy is released when very light neutrino bombards the nucleus of an atom and by splitting it into two smaller parts it releases up to 200 times the energy, as the missing mass of the nucleus.

Fusion energy is released when two lighter atomic nuclei fuse to form a heavier nucleus and some of the mass is converted to energy in the form of heat, light, sound and electricity. The energy/force produced by nuclear bombs was first applied in World War II. It started with the atomic or fission bomb. The second generation thermonuclear weapons or hydrogen bombs use fusion to start the fission process. Other types of nuclear bombs have been developed, like the neutron bomb, mainly to release the deadly radiation. As an example, the energy released and the amount of force produced by 2400 pound fission bomb is over 1.2 million tons. Fusion power could provide more safe energy than any other source currently in use. The problem is that until a more economical production method is discovered, it takes more energy to produce it than the fusion energy received. The primary fuel for producing fusion energy is deuterium. There is unlimited amount of deuterium in the seawater and it could become the future energy source for human civilization after all the fossil fuels have been depleted. Radioactive decay is energy when unstable atomic nucleus loses energy by emitting ionizing particles and radiation. Max Plank Institute of Plasma physics stellator, called Wendelstein 7-x produced the first helium plasma on Dec. 19, 2015, and on Feb. 3, 2016 the first hydrogen plasma. Stellator is a device used to confine hot plasma with magnetic fields for controlled nuclear reaction.

There are many hypothetical theories about the "Dark energy". The 2004 Chamelon theory of scalar particles and the 2013 Pressuron theory of string dilation are some of the latest hypothesis. Dark energy has repulsive force causing the expansion of the observable universe. However, if the galaxies are moving away from the earth faster then the speed of light, they are not observable. The expansion of the universe by the Hubble's law is called Hubble flow, based on the latest Hubble constant of 67.80 Mpc. The report of the Planck spacecraft Mar. 21, 2013 observation concluded: Universe contains 68.3 % of dark energy. Without understanding what it is, the present concurrence is: Dark energy is everywhere in the space. Scientists have no explanation for the existence of dark energy or mass velocity beyond the speed of light. The only logical answer is: It is God's force/energy.

7 | Cosmic Radiation

The controversy of particle vs. wave started with Sir Isaac Newton's (1642-1727 CE) particle theory by combining it with the pulsation dynamics. It was Newton who started the scientific revolution, honored as the most influential scientist of all time. He was the President of Royal Society of London (PRS) until his death. He believed in creation and wrote volumes on theological and biblical subjects. His passion was to unite the Book of Scriptures with the Book of Nature. After writing about the Law of Gravitation, he changed the particle theory to wave theory. The wave-particle controversy of light has been debated for centuries. Maxwell (1831-1879 CE) converted it back to particle theory, then Hertz (1857-1894 CE) and then Plank's (1858-1947

CE) postulated radiation formulae of "Quantum of Energy = h Times Frequency" and his theory of "Constant Motion of Particles in Circles". Einstein (1879-1955 CE) published his theory of "Light is a continuous wave, but consisted of localized particles" in 1905. This was his explanation: "It seems as though we must use sometimes the one theory and sometimes the other, while at times we may use either. We are faced with a new kind of difficulty. We have two contradictory pictures of reality; separately neither of them fully explains the phenomena of light, but together they do". Einstein received Nobel prize in 1921 for his theory of photons and photoelectric effect of light. This was confirmed by Millikan (1868-1953 CE), followed by Plank and Bohr (1885-1962 CE) who completely destroyed Maxwell's theory of particles. Pauli (1900-1958 CE) discovered the fourth mysterious quantum number in 1945 and proposed that "phase" waves move faster than light. Then De Broglie's (1892-1987 CE) idea that matter, made up from particles like electrons, must be accompanied by waves. So, the "Quantum Theory" was born with photons and electrons dealing with the interaction of matter and radiation in an atomic or molecular scale. Free electrons from atoms and molecules transmit ionized radiation energy, which are carried by waves. The electromagnetic waves are the disturbance propagating energy through a medium from low radio waves to visible waves to high gamma rays. Cosmologists are relying on probabilities when arriving on the accuracy of the electron anomalous magnetic dipole moment. The use of mathematical formulas, without knowing what the Quantum Electrodynamics (QE) is or where the QE came from, is still an unsolved mystery. Mar. 2, 2015 experiment by researchers at Ecole Polytechique Federale de Lausanne showed wave-particle nature of light wave. A few years ago scientists started to use the wave-particle duality of light in electron microscopy and neutron diffraction without really understanding it. To this day the wave-particle and the electromagnetic radiation theories are only postulates based on hypothetical assumptions. Light (photon) is mass-less, but acts as a particle. Since waves are the source for all fields, cosmologists have now proclaimed

EVERY ELEMENTARY PARTICLE or QUANTIC ENTITY has a WAVE DUALITY NATURE. Also, the Quantum Field Theories (QFT) are incomplete without adding "hidden " variables. The hypothetical physical phenomena of QFT is based on probability and remains the most difficult theory in modern physics. If the QE "fields" are continuous waves transmitted from energy sources in the masses, how can it retain the mass without losing particles in the wave?

To confirm the "theory" of the Big Bang, ESA (European Space Agency) launched on Dec. 3, 2015, LISA (Laser Interferometer Space Antennae) Pathfinder on a Vega rocket from Europe's Spaceport in Kourou, French Guiana. The original LISA program was a joint space mission with ESA to observe gravitational waves and geodesic motion, but the funding to NASA was cut off and USA participation was cancelled . This LISA launch will be used to test the technologies for the "evolved" LISA (eLISA) observatory panned for 2034 launch. This observatory will consist of three spacecrafts arranged in equilateral triangle to detect any stochastic or unpredictable background of gravitational waves.

Cosmologists believe that primordial gravitational waves from the Big Bang can be observed in the Cosmic Microwave Background (CMB) radiation after the recombination epoch, when electrons and protons formed the first hydrogen atoms and released free photons into universe. The problem is, observation from the radio telescopes shows that CMB radiation comes from all directions, but Big Bang should have only one single point source. Einstein predicted the effects of gravitational waves in the 1916 theory of General Relativity as "Ripples or curvature in the spacetime". The cosmologists were hoping to detect CMB by observing primordial electromagnetic radiation with weak gravitational lensing. It was Einstein's idea to use gravitational lensing back in 1912, but he did not think that it can become observational reality until Rudi Mandl contacted him and asked him to submit the mathematical equation to the Science News letter in Dec. 19, 1936. The research with gravitational lensing discovered the twin quasars (Twin QSO) in 1979 and then the four objects in the universe from one single object, which was named the "Einstein Cross". March 17,

2014 report claimed that BICEP2 (Background Imaging of Cosmic Extragalatic Polarization) instruments at South Pole detected B-modes or cosmic inflation from the gravitational waves in the early universe. But this report was wrong. Jan. 30, 2015 announcement changed the result of this observation from cosmic inflation to interstellar dust. On Feb. 11, 2016 authors of the Advanced LIGO (Laser Interferometer Gravitational-wave Observatory) collaboration published the results of the separation of signals by 7 milliseconds between the L1 detector in Livingstone, Louisiana and the H1 detector in Hanford, Washington of the Sep. 14, 2015 observation of two black holes with 29 and 36 solar masses merging together 1.3 billion light years ago and releasing 3 solar masses as gravitational waves. One solar mass is equal to the mass of our sun. These detectors were 3002 kilometers apart and the difference in signals received by the detectors followed Einstein's Gravitational waves theory in General Relativity. However, cosmologists continue to research the polarization of the CMB radiation hoping to discover the hypothetical B-modes or cosmic inflation.

According to Andre Linde feigned theory of inflation, or faster tan the speed of light, the expansion of the universe in less than a trillionth of a second after the Big Bang, the polarization of CMB should have produced gravitational waves observable on earth. But, to this date NO gravitational waves from the single source of the Big Bang have been detected! If gravity or gravitation was part of the Big Bang "fundamental" force, it is still a mystery. Scientists have been unable to discover the hypothetical "graviton" particles or the source of them. They call gravity mass/energy between two bodies and not a force. Gravitation is part of Einstein's "Space-time" theory in General Relativity, adding time, or objects velocity relative to the observer, to the three physical dimensions and the universal gravitational constant "G". The 2013 theory of "Pressuron" claims that gravitation is not an attractive force between masses, but "pressure-force" exerted by space-time on closed volumes (masses) that tend to bring them closer to each other. The problem with the Big Bang theory is, it should have a single point source, but in the abstract universe the CMB radiation comes from all directions and gains twice as much energy as expected. These facts completely invalidate the Big Bang and inflation hypothesis. Also, if the wave-particle duality is true, then the waves transmitting them in the universe contain energy/mass and the space is NOT A VACUUM, as proposed by the Heisenber's Uncertainty Principle. To transmit energy/mass and maintain a completely empty vacuum is impossible. For vacuum energy of space see THE SECRETS OF COSMOS article.

Democritus (460 to 370 BCE), the ancient Greek philosopher, was the first to formulate the atomic theory of the universe and is considered to be the father of the modern science. Another ancient Greek philosopher Aristotle (384 to 322 BCE) believed that the cosmos beyond the moon consisted of the fifth element "aether", presently called ether. His theory of the light in the cosmos was the wave-like phenomenon seen through luminiferous ether. Whether it is ether, dark energy or God's energy, cosmos can only exist with force/energy. The question is: What was the source of this incalculable amount energy?

8

Spiritual Information of Matter

Commonly assumed tenet of science is: "In principle complete information about a physical system at one point of time should determine its state at any other time". Another words, information resolves uncertainty and cannot be lost. In 1975 Hawking and Reckenstein predicted that a slow radiation from black holes will cause information loss. It was due to quantum effects near the event horizon known as the "Hawking radiation". However, this was in violation of unitarity and contrary to the preservation of information contained in the principles of quantum determinism and reversibility. Jan. 24, 2014 article in Nature reported that Hawking had changed his theory and he now believes that information is not lost in black holes. In the quantum theory, energy and information can escape from black hole when gravity merges with other fundamental forces. However, there is no proof for a fundamental or unified force. The claim by Hawking that information can pass through the black hole in a wormhole into a parallel universe is even less provable. The Jan. 8, 2016 postulate for information being saved in "soft" photons and gravitons is one of the hypothetical versions of zero energy subatomic particles existing in zero energy space. In the string theory version, the information could depart from the black hole entropy. Hawking has again corrected his hypothesis and now claims that there are NO EVENT HORIZONS, only an "Apparent horizon" without any singularity.

The unsolved mystery is: Does the "Fundamental Force" contain all the information in the present universe from the beginning of the hypothetical Big Bang, or was the information added later? From Einstein's theory of Energy/force = Mass/matter x speed of light squared, the converse is "MATTER equals FORCE/speed of light squared". According to the Standard Model (SM) theory, all matter is made from QUARKS or the smallest hypothetical elementary particles. Cosmologists have not determined how the quarks originated or at what point the information caused the formation of composite particles with protons and neutrons called hadrons. Quarks are classified by their flavor or electric and color charge, spin and mass with gluon particle field and identified by their quantum number. Quarks are not found in isolation and according to the inherent information, comprised in two types of hadrons. One is called Masons, consisting of one quark and one anti-quark and the other is Baryons, consisting of three quarks. The charged Masons decay into negatively charged electrons and uncharged Mesons decay into photons. Baryons are positively charged protons. When strong force holds the protons together with neutrons, which have no electrical charge, they form the nucleolus of an atom. Electrons and neutrinos, called leptons, are subject to weak interaction, gravitation and electromagnetic forces. Leptons, gauge bosons and hypothetical gravitons have no quarks or baryon numbers. There are four gauge bosons, or force carriers.

1) The photons carry the electromagnetic force

2) The hypothetical W and Z particles and the electromagnetic force is combined with

3) The weak force now called "Electroweak" force, and

4) The gluon or strong interaction is the nuclear force, plus the decay of Higgs boson, which was discovered on July 4, 2012 by scientists at LHC.

Cosmologists have not defined the cause for the birth of the universe or the source for the Big Bang Fundamental force. This fundamental or unified force appeared out of nothing and included all four forces, plus gravity. They further hypothesized that the whole early universe was filled with very high density energy under extremely high temperatures and pressure. After the universe cooled the "quark-gluon plasma", or the most abundant visible matter in the universe, appeared out of nowhere. If the first elements were created during the primordial nucleosynthesis, then there is no need for the hypothetical Higgs field with Higgs bosons for adding mass to subatomic particles. But the hypothetical Higgs field is everywhere in the universe continually interacting with quarks, charged leptons and W &Z bosons by imparting "mass" through electroweak interaction. If the source for the plasma was Big Bang, or the Higgs field or God's energy, it remains an unsolvable mystery. There is no proof for the recombination theory of the original hydrogen atoms forming without a cause by itself out of elementary particles and gauge bosons. The primordial deuterium atoms were destroyed by the high temperature, and cosmologists named the process DEUTERIUM BOTTLENECK. Before the protons of the hydrogen atom fuse to form helium atom with two protons held together by the strong nuclear force, stellar supernova nucleosynthesis transmutes one proton into neutron in beta decay, called quantum tunneling. But this process is not possible under the classical physics! In beta decay the nucleus emits antineutrino electrons or positrons via the weak interaction and balances the atoms positively charged protons with the negatively charged electrons. The appearance of the weak interaction and the strong nuclear forces are caused by the fictitious gravitational force, containing the spiritual information. The universe has over hundred billion trillion stars with planets, inter-stellar and inter-galactic media consisting of infinite number of atoms. The visible matter in the universe is comprised with 111 known elements and 7 hypothetical elements, plus isotopes. The element number is based on equal amount of positively charged protons and negatively charged electrons. Elements with less electrons than the number of protons are positively charged "cations" and with more electrons than the number of protons are negatively charged "anions".

In 1920-s Heidelberg and Bohr postulated the Quantum Mechanics theory, later called the Copenhagen Interpretation. It included many different views on wave functions and subatomic processes. Bohr's theory was that a particle was separate from the wave, while Heidelberg proposed a wave-particle duality. Einstein opposed the Copenhagen interpretation because it was not adequate for quantum theory and it contradicted his Special relativity theory. In

1935 Einstein and his colleagues Podolsky and Rosen challenged the particles inherent knowledge in the quantum theory, better known as EPR Paradox. The challenge stated that the wave function does not indicate physical reality and it is impossible to know both the position and the momentum of the particle without hidden variables. Einstein's comment was "I, at any rate, am convinced that He or God does not throw dice" and "Do you really think that the moon isn't there , if you aren't looking at it?" If you want to measure both, one particle's position and momentum with a conjugate particle more accurately than is possible under the Heidelberg's uncertainity principle, then signaling must be faster than the speed of light. This EPR paradox is now called the Quantum Entanglement, challenging the undetermined action of the subatomic particles and the impossibility of faster than the speed of light signaling. There is no known method to verify the position and the momentum of the quantum particle at any time.

It is irrational to believe that all the elements in the universe were caused by chance and accidentally formed the visible universe. Either the particles had inherent information to form the atoms, molecules and all forms of matter, or it was preordained design controlled by outside source. In both cases it can be only by God, the creator of the universe.

9

Fictitious Antimatter Atoms

The Antiparticles Theories

In the Standard Model (SM) theory every known particle has an antiparticle with an opposite charge and spin. Elementary particles have an intrinsic quantum mechanical property called "spin". Spin is the quantum version of angular momentum. The fundamental or Dirac Fermions, or matter particles, have half-integer spin and fundamental Bosons, or force particles, have integer spin. Marjorana fermions with zero charge are their own antiparticles, except neutrinos or neutral leptons. According to the latest SM theory, the visible matter in the universe is the accidental surplus of matter over the antimatter. Scientists call it "Baryogenesis", or the hypothetical process that produced the imbalance between baryons and antibaryons. Baryons consist of 3 up or down quarks and anti-baryons with 3 opposite up or down quarks. Baryons and mesons are part of the hadrons, called baryonic or building matter of the universe. Mesons are composed of one quark and one antiquark. Antiquarks are effected by the strong or nuclear force lasting up to a few hundredths of microseconds before annihilated. All subatomic particles also have antiparticles. The protons have antiprotons, neutrons have antineutrons, electrons have positrons, etc. Mesons transport nuclear force and may decay into electrons, neutrinos or protons. However, there are no hypothetical heavy mesons in the universe left from the Big Bang (BB) or the primordial nucleosynthesis, which was the source for the initial hydrogen atom with one proton and one neutron nucleus.

The "Quark epoch" in SM theory started in picosecond, or one trillionth of a second after the BB, when the four forces separated from the "Fundamental" force. The homogenous universe was filled with very high density energy, huge temperature and pressure. After one millionth of a second, when the cooling of the universe temperature allowed quarks to bind together, the "Hadron epoch" began. Most hadrons/anti-hadrons were eliminated in annihilation reaction, and when the universe further cooled the "Lepton epoch" began one second after the BB. When most of the leptons and anti-leptons were annihilated in about 10 seconds, leaving a small residue of leptons after the end of lepton epoch, the universe consisted of hot quark-gluon plasma and quarks became confined within the hadrons. After the hypothetical baryogenesis the next step was nucleosynthesis. It began with "Photon epoch" within 10 seconds to 20 minutes after BB, when protons and neutrons formed the nuclei of the first atom Hydrogen (Atomic number 1). Atomic number of an element is the same as the number of protons in the nuclei of atoms. During the first few minutes of the photon epoch the assumption is that in addition to hydrogen-1 deuterium (hydrogen isotope), most amount of amount of helium (atomic number 2), and a small amount of lithium (atomic number 3) were created. Atoms with equal number of protons and electrons, became dominant over charged particles about 380 years after BB. Universe contained hot dense plasma of nuclei, electrons and photons until 379 years after BB, until the temperature was low enough for nuclei to combine with electrons and create neutral atoms. Scientists have now discovered 94 elements, which occur on earth naturally, plus 24 synthetic elements , total of 118 elements. 38 elements have exclusively radio-active isotopes, which decay over time into other elements. All elements have isotopes, or atoms with the same number of photons and electrons, but different number of neutrons in the nuclei of atom. Only 80 elements have stable isotopes, the rest are unstable. Most of the elements on earth are chemical compounds, only 32 are without the mix of other elements. Primordial isotopes are the product of stellar nucleosynthesis or caused by cosmic rays spallation. Galatic cosmic ray spallation is naturally occurring nuclear fission, when cosmic rays or high energy proton strikes an atomic nucleus in the interstellar medium. Isotopes are used in radiometric dating and in nuclear medicine. The best known uses are the radiocarbon dating, several forms of spectroscopy and in a Positron Emission Tomography (PET) scanning equipment.

Atoms are either positive ions called "Cations", when they have either less negative charged electrons than the number of positive charged protons, or with more electrons than the number of protons, then called negative ions or "Anions". Cations and anions with opposite electrical charges attract each other and readily form ionic compounds, like salts and plasma. Plasma is one of the four fundamental states of matter with properties unlike solid, liquid or gas. The neutral charged plasma, with positive and negative charged ions, can only exist through ionization. Plasma is the most common phase of ordinary or bayonic matter in the universe. Plasma is a complex system, either found in nature or created by artificial process. There are dozens of fields of active research on plasma, including the mystery of the cellular structure of space.

Scientists have been researching "Electron Magnetic and Electric Dipole Moments".

Electron spin in an atom produces magnetic field called "Magnetic Moment". Electron and positron "Magnetic Dipole Moment" (MDM) is caused by the intrinsic properties of electron spin and electric charge. In Quantum Electrodynamics (QED) theory the light and matter interact for Anomalous Magnetic Moment (AMM). Composite particles have huge amount of AMM, like protons, antiprotons and neutrons. The AMM differs slightly from the latest Gabrielse Group observed EDM value of 7.6 parts in ten trillion.

Electron "Electric Dipole Moment" (EDM) is the measure of the separation of positive and negative electrical charge, or dipole of the intrinsic property of electron in a system's overall polarity. It is the charge times the distance between them, from the negative side towards the positive side or a vector quantity measurement of non-zero EDM of the electron. The research for Charge Parity (CP) and Time (T) violations by Gabrielse Group and by many others have found NO NON-ZERO EDM! Also, in strong interaction between quarks and gluons in protons, neutrons and pions of the hadrons family, the Quantum Chromodynamics (QCD) theory did not disclose any invariance in EDM. Pions are mesons, the carriers of strong force, consisting of a quark and an antiquark. The three CPT-symmetry violations, with time reversal invariance, mean that neutrons can have no EDM, a property implying the separation of the internal charges. The universe is governed by certain fundamental symmetries and the reversal of time requires completely new physics, which is not possible under the existing interactions in the electroweak theory.

The Antimatter Atoms

To this date NO NATURAL or PRIMORDIAL ANTIMATTER ATOMS have ever been observed. There is NO BARYOGENESIS and NO LEFT-OVER atoms in the cosmos! Karl Pearson proposed in 1880's the existence of fourth dimension with the flow from negative matter or "Sinks" to "aether" or normal matter "Squirts". In 2002 The ATHENA project announced they had created the first "cold" ANTIHYDROGEN atom. In November 2010 ALPHA Collaboration announced the trapping of 309 ANTIHYDROGEN atoms for 17 minutes. Jan. 22, 2014 CERN antimatter experiment at LHC produced the first beam of 80 antihydrogen atoms. Data now released by CERN to produce 1 mole or 1.008 grams of antihydrogen would take 100 billion years and cost $65.5 trillion in present day US currency. Although all subatomic particles have antiparticles, there are no natural anti-atoms. If baryogenesis could create any antimatter atoms or new anti-atoms by cosmic rays spallation , they would immediately annihilate with the visible matter. By creating large amounts of synthetic antimatter atoms, there is a real possibility of causing a chain reactions and immediately annihilate all matter in the universe.

There is no physical proof for BB, nor the dark matter or the primordial nucleosynthesis. Cosmologists keep an eerie silence on the origin of the "Fundamental Force" and the appearance of the incomprehensible amount of "Quark-gluon Plasma" proposed in SM theory. Also, no explanation for the source of the very high density energy, huge temperature and pressure in "Quark epoch". If Nucleosynthesis is a process of creating new atomic nuclei from the pre-existing nucleons, when were the pre-exiting nucleons created?

The BB in SM theory describes a "Fundamental force out of nowhere accidentally discovered an infinite universe and without a cause, out of nothing, by itself, generated over one hundred billion trillion stars with planets, interstellar and intergalatic media". The Higgs field, dark energy and quark-gluon plasma being everywhere in the universe remains a mystery. It can only exist with the energy/force from God, who created all the matter/antimatter in the cosmos.

10

The Mass of the Universe

When converting Einstein's theory of $E=mc^2$ to $m=E/c^2$, or mass equals energy and delete the speed of light squared, then the mass is Energy or $m=E$. In the Standard Model (SM) theory the visible mass created by the Big Bang was the hot quark-gluon plasma, a matter which is everywhere in the universe. However, the discovery of Higgs bosons at the Large Hadron Collider (LHC) and the hypothetical Higgs field "imparting" mass through electroweak interaction to all subatomic particles, is the latest hypothesis for the visible matter. The LHC was built by European Organization for Nuclear Research or CERN. It is a 27 kilometer tunnel near Geneva Switzerland with the following seven detectors at different underground locations:

1. ATLAS detects origins of mass and extra dimensions for new physics.

2. CMS detects Higgs bosons and fictitious dark matter.

3. ALICE detects quark-gluon plasma, or "fluid" form of matter

4. LHCb researching the "missing" antimatter and the fictitious dark matter

5,6 & 7. TOTEM, McEDAL and LHCf for specialized research

Initial testing for first creation of quark-gluon plasma on was on Nov. 20, 2009. The SM theory relies on the Higgs boson or God's particles, the first scalar particle in nature and the building blocks of the universe. The July 4, 2012 initial discovery of Higgs boson decay with ATLAS and CMS experiments at LHC was confirmed on March 14, 2013. The Higgs boson had a mass of 125.3 GeV/c² giga (billion) electron volts. However, to provide mass to all the other particles in the universe and to support the SM theory, the mass of the Higgs bosons should be billions of times more than the one discovered at LHC.

Mesons are subatomic particles consisting of one quark and one antiquark. However, the Apr. 14, 2014 CERN discovery of exotic state hadrons with two quarks and two anti-quarks and the July 14, 2015 discovery of new, never before observed Pentaquarks are invalidating all previous theories of charged mesons decaying into electrons and neutrinos, or the uncharged mesons decaying into photons. Aug. 8, 2015 CERN experiment revealed that the masses of the proton and antiproton are identical. This fact proves that matter and antimatter particles in the universe are EQUAL. Also, the Aug. 30, 2015 CERN study invalidated the SM prediction by revealing that leptons violate the subatomic particles interaction. The first ion collisions test was made on Nov. 25, 2015 at record breaking energy of more than 1 PeV. The Dec. 15, 2015 preliminary test results revealed new subatomic particles, including candidates for gravitons and the heavier Higgs bosons to validate the Higgs field. CERN continues the exotic search for other hypothetical subatomic particles like

"Tachyon", "Chameleon", "Axion", etc, and for super-symmetry (SUSY). The SUSY theory adds hypothetical super-partners to all bosons and fermions and provides the necessary mass to all the particles in the universe, but this doubling of the number of particles completely invalidates the SM theory. There is no compelling evidence for trachyon or tau netrino particles moving faster than the speed of light. It violates the Casualty theory in the Special Relativity and the initial claim for it was withdrawn by CERN. Also, no superpartners with bosons and fermions have been observed, and if SUSY can exist, it must be spontaneously broken symmetry to allow the difference in mass. The SM does not explain gravity, dark energy and contains many other anomalies on the creation of mass. a) Possibly five separate Higgs bosons, b) Unparticles physics, c) Hypothetical technicolor force, d) The Higgs boson is not the final particle, it is comprised of even smaller "particles" than quarks.

To validate their hypothesis scientists invent hypothetical and virtual elementary particles, usually named after the inventor. Starting with the elusive graviton particle, which remains a mystery. The untested Chameleon scalar particles are the postulated fifth force for the dark energy expansion of the universe. The SM predicts new particles called WIMP's (Weakly Interactive Massive Particles) that interact with electroweak force known as "WIMP miracle", but all experiments have failed to discover this fictitious dark matter particle. The axion elementary particle is postulated to resolve the Charge Parity(CP) problem in Chromodynamics (QCD), if it exists at all. The appearance of Nambu-Goldstone bosons in models exhibiting "Spontaneous breakdown" of continuous symmetries, is the conjectural trigger for Higgs mechanism.

The problem of reconciling quantum theory of gravity with general relativity remains unsolvable. Heisenberg's "Uncertainty Principle" (UP) provides a new way of explaining how atoms behave. Quantum theory proposed that energy was not continuous, but came in discrete packets (quanta) and light could be described as both, a wave and a stream of quanta. This idea is now a fundamental part of the quantum description of the cosmos. According to the UP, the position

(x) and the momentum (p) of a particle cannot be measured with absolute precision. The more accurate is one measure, the less accurate is the other measure. By applying UP many things can be observed and discovered, which cannot be explained by the classical non-quantum physics. A process known as "Quantum tunneling", a particle tunnels through a barrier that it classically could not surpass. The phenomena applies to nuclear fusion sequence in stars, quantum computing, scanning tunneling microscope, and others. Although this is nothing more than conjecture, it is part of the present "scientific" formulae.

One of the major problems in science is the quantum gravity. Quantum gravity is not compatible with general relativity theory. Cosmologists are trying to unify gravity with the other fundamental forces in the hypothetical 10 String theory, with nine dimensions plus one dimension of time, and with "Loop quantum gravity" theory, which quantizes the gravitational field. In the string theory the zero dimensional subatomic point-like particles, or hadrons are made of one-dimensional strings that vibrate at the speed of light. The frequency of vibration matches the mass of the particle. There are five different hypothesis for the six additional strings to the four-dimensional universe of length, width, height and space-time. To overcome the variances in the extra six strings hypothesis, cosmologists added another string to the ten-dimensional universe and called the eleven string universe M-theory or the Theory of Everything (TOE), where quantum gravity is unified with all the known forces. None of the experiments on these hypothesis, however, have produced any credible evidence for realistic existence.

Cosmologists keep an eerie silence about any phenomena they have no explanation or solution. Starting with a) The source of the "Fundamental" force for BB, b) The astronomical amount of energy and high temperature after the BB, c) The appearance of mass for quark-gluon plasma without Higgs field, d) The existence of Higgs field throughout universe, e) The incalculable amount of energy=mass to create over hundred billion trillion stars with planets, interstellar and intergalatic media.

The Uncertainty Principle (UP) in physics is the cosmologists most accurate formula for explaining the fundamental limit to human knowledge of atoms, light and vacuum. They can calculate the probabilities where things are and how they will behave, but without any idea why. How UP is balancing the positive nucleus and the negative electrons with electroweak force in atoms. The most eccentric result of UP is the inherent certainty of NO vacuum or absence of everything in the quantum processes. The UP equation also applies to energy and time, the more time is confined, the less confined is the system's energy. The appearance of "Virtual particles" for nanoseconds in the vacuum and then annihilating with their antiparticles is a quantum physics hypothesis for life. Without these virtual or not veritable particles life will not exist at all. The transmission of light and radiation under quantum process can also be expressed in terms of energy and time. It is ironic that the scientists explain the existence of mass in the universe with the Uncertainty Principle. Since the creation of mass has no provable origin without God's creation, it is appropriate to call it uncertain.

11

The Secrets of Cosmos

The earth's location in the Milky Way galaxy's minor arm of Orion gives us an excellent view to study the cosmos. The mean distance of earth from the sun is149,597,871 kilometers or 92,955,807 miles, or one Astronomical Unit (AU). Our solar system starts with the closest planet to the sun Mercury, then Venus and then our planet Earth, followed by Mars. Between Mars and Jupiter is the asteroid belt, which is followed by Saturn, Uranus and Neptune. Beyond the orbit of Neptune is the Kuiper belt with trans-Neptunian objects (TNO's) consisting of rocks, ice, methane and ammonia. One of the best known objects is Pluto, first classified as a planet, but now called planetoid. Pluto is a rock and ice TNO orbiting 30 - 49

AU's from the sun. Beyond the Kuiper belt is the "Scattered Disc" belt of countless minor icy planets or planetoids. The largest planetoid is Eris, approximately 96.6 AU's from the sun. The hypothetical Hills or Oort cloud is beyond the Scatted Disc belt containing icy planetesimals or very small fractions of planets.

Cosmologists have been searching the universe hoping to find planets with water and any signs of life. Although water in the form of ice is the second most abundant element in the universe, no present or past carbon-based life has been discovered. Their research revealed only signs of past chemical reactions between elements, but this is not life. Life requires complex molecules of proteins, nucleic acids, carbohydrates and lipids. It is our earth, with 70% surface water, which is the only suitable planet for human life in our solar system. Cosmologists have discovered over 2000 exoplanets or planets outside our solar system. Observation of all exoplanets showed extremely hostile conditions not suitable for supporting carbon-based life. Cosmologists named them "Hell worlds". Water is absolutely necessary for carbon-based life and finding ice on exoplanets or planetoids does not mean that there can be or ever has been life anywhere else in the universe. There are over 200 other critical elements and conditions required for any intelligent life to exist. First, the distance from the sun is critical for life to exist on earth. This provides perfect temperature range for water (H_2O) to form as liquid, ice or gas. The density of water is lower in the solid form (ice) and much lower in the form of gas. The maximum density of water is 4°C (39°F) and it changes into ice at temperatures lower than 4°C. The ice raises to the surface of water thereby saving our lakes and rivers from freezing into solid ice. H_2O molecules have a special type of electrostatic attraction with intermolecular force designed for our existence. Some of the other requirements are itemized in the INCONCEIVABLE EXISTENCE chapter. Astrophysicists do not know how the planets were formed or when the solar system was created. Our large moon, compared to the size of earth, is the most unique feature not found in any other planetary system. Without our large moon human life on earth would not be possible. See the article on REALISTIC THEORY OF GALAXIES covering the creation of our sun and the planets.

According to the latest estimates by astrophysicists, there are over one hundred billion trillion (100, 000,000,000,000,000,000,000+) stars in the observable universe. Total visible matter in the universe is 4%, the rest of the 96% is empty space. In the 4% visible matter 5.9% are stars, 1.7% is the interstellar matter (planets and belts) and the rest of 92.4% is the intergalatic matter (nebulae and dust). The stars are classified as A (white, bluish white), O & B (blue), F & G (yellow to white), K &M (orange to red), L ,T&Y (red to brown dwarf), D (white dwarf), R (red dwarf to giant), S (red and blue super-giant) and WR (Wolf-Rayset). Most common stars are the main sequence G class stars and the M class stars. Our sun is G2V class yellow dwarf hydrogen star. The larger the star the quicker it burns the hydrogen and the shorter the life span of the star. Nearly 97% of the main sequence stars life span ends when the inner core of the star fuses into carbon and oxygen and then expands into a red giant. When the carbon is fused to neon and then to iron, the star explodes in supernova and the inner core collapses into a white dwarf. The outer burning shell of the star is expelled outwards creating interstellar media, including the colorful nebulae. As an example, when the original star had the mass like our sun, the white dwarf will only have the mass of our earth. There are seven (A, B, C, O, Q, X and Z) spectral types of white dwarfs, plus four (E, H, P and V) secondary features. All white dwarfs are D class stars, 80% designated as DA type, 16% as DB type and 4% the remaining five types. When the class D white dwarf stars start to lose all their energy and brightness, they finally end up as black dwarfs. Cosmologists have observed white dwarf stars older than the 13.83 light year universe. What happens at the end of stars life depends mostly on the size of the star or the solar mass of the star. One solar mass is equal to the mass of our sun, or about million trillion trillion kilograms (30 zeros). As an example, if the original star had a million kilometer radius, it will compact into a neutron or class W star with 11 kilometer radius. These stars have the most dense mass and according to astrophysicists calculations one ounce of neutron star mass may weigh millions of tons on earth. Neutron stars with strong magnetic field are called magnetars and the rotating neutron stars are called pulsars by emitting X-rays and gamma rays. Astrophysicists think that collapsars and microquasar are binary stars with a normal O, B, A, F,&G type stars and a compact object, emitting x-rays and gamma rays. They think that these objects are candidates for stellar black holes or small neutron stars. Since the stellar black holes are only an unproven postulate, the probable cause for the radiation is a small neutron star with very heavy mass, detected by synchrotron radio emission. The hypothetical neutron stars with exotic matter are called the Q stars. K, M, S stars and most class C carbon stars change to RGB and AGB red giant stars and then explode in hypernovae. The galaxies and the intergalatic media was created within a few million years after the primordial super giant star cores fused into heavier elements and then exploded in hypernovae. This explosion spread the unburned hydrogen and all the heavier elements throughout the galaxies leaving a super massive black hole in the centers of all galaxies. Read the REALISTIC THEORY OF GALAXIES chapter for additional details. The hypothesis for the enormous energy of Black holes is the postulared gravitational singularity. It is one-dimensional single point in the center of the black hole containing huge mass of gravity with infinite density and infinitely curved space-time beyond the laws of present physics.

Cosmologists agree that the magnitude of the "Dark energy" or "Vacuum energy of space" on the cosmological scale is too low to cause the expansion of the universe. They call this dilemma "Vacuum catastrophe! "It should have at least 10,113 more joules than postulated in the "Spontaneous Emission" theory of Cashmir effect and in the Lamb shift. A joul (J) is a unit of energy to accelerate one kilogram of mass at a rate of one meter per second. In spontaneous emission when matter is in exited state it emits energy and thereby changing to a lower energy level. "Simulated Emission" is when photon interacts with exited electron causing the lower energy level. The present vacuum energy hypothesis, with virtual pairs of particles, one negatively charged and one positively charged particle existing only a fraction of a second before annihilating each other, can produce only an infinitesimally small amount of energy. To this date NO VACUUM ENERGY particles have been observed, nor is the source of this energy established. The amount of dark or vacuum energy required to surpass the force of gravity and to expand the universe is immeasurable. If particles annihilation releases only energy in the vacuum, it completely ignores the requirement for a media to transmit waves in the space. The paradox is: The physical reality of De Broglie waves has never been proven. The quantum decoherence of irreversible wave function collapse is immeasurable and cannot be proven experimentally. The "Copenhagen Interpretation" declares that the underlying reality in unknowable and beyond the present scientific reality. This idea was originally proposed by Einstein in the quantum mechanics. The presently accepted Heisengerg's "Uncertainty Principle" is inherent in all wave-like systems. In the quantum tunneling theory anything is possible under the uncertainty principle. Read THE MASS OF THE UNIVERSE chapter for more details.

The tiniest subatomic particles are called neutrinos or neutral leptons. Neutrinos are created in nuclear reactions and in supernovae. The radioactive decay of neutrinos from supernovae are transmitted by cosmic rays. The electron neutrinos are the first generation of leptons, the muon neutrinos are the second generation of leptons and the tau neutrinos are the third generation of leptons. Leptons and quarks are the building block of the matter. Neutrinos can oscillate from one generation to the next generation only if they have mass, but neutrino mass is still unknown. The most common neutrinos observed on earth are the electron or solar neutrinos. Our sun transmits over 60 billion neutrinos per second to every square centimeter on earth. The virtual mass of neutrinos and photons existing in the universe are part of the mysterious "Vacuum" or "Dark" energy particles.

12 | Accident or Predetermination

Using radiometric dating method scientists have estimated the age of the earth to be 4.54 billion years old, plus or minus 0.05 billion. It was a violent time in earth's history, called the Hadean era, lasting half a billion years. It was followed by Eoarchea era with the discover of 4.1 billion year old rocks in Western Australia. These are the oldest remains of biotic life on earth. LUCA (Last universal common ancestors) or the first single cell organism appeared on earth about 3.6 billion of years ago. Scientists are using thermoluminar or optical infrared stimulated luminescence dating methods to measure the energy of photons released from quartz or potassium Feldspar on the earth crust, for estimating how long ago these silicate minerals were formed on earth. This is more positive method of dating the ages than the generally used measure of carbon 14 decay. The accelerator mass spectrometry method detects and counts the C14 atoms directly and is more reliable than measuring the decay. There are uranium-thorium, rubidium-strontium (lead), potassium-argon and other dating methods depending on the matter to be dated.

In the history of earth there has been over 10 ice ages or glaciations and 5 major extinctions with up to 96% life being destroyed. Climatologists estimate that there are many extinctions of species every year called Holocene extinction. The Cambrian explosion started about 543 million years ago and lasted 53 million years with four major extinctions. There was no life on dry land and most of the aquatic life was destroyed by glaciations. This era was called Proterozoic eon, when one single supercontinent Rodinia broke into two new continents. 1. The Gondwana continent, which later divided into Africa, Australia, South America and Southern Asia, and 2. Laurentia continent, the present North America, part of Europe and north

Asia. The Permian-Triassic extinction about 251 million years ago was most devastating event on earth when 96% of all life was exterminated. The Cretaceous-Paleogene extinction about 66 million years ago also killed over 76% of life on earth. The specific reasons for each extinction are still undetermined. It could have been caused by asteroids or comets, volcanic and tectonic action, glaciations and climate changes, or combination of any of them. But every time new and different life forms appeared almost immediately after each extinction. Geneticists have been unable to substantiate that evolution had sufficient time for a modern human or Homo sapiens sapiens, to appear on earth after the last Cretaceous extinction 66 million years ago. It is either a miracle or creation by God. Even Stephen Hawking, the famous cosmologist, called the human life on earth "A LUCKY BREAK!" Geneticists estimate for the "evolution" of Homo sapiens sapiens from atoms to a modern man required "infinite" amount of time.

Charles Darwin (1809-1882) was the instigator of the natural selection theory and the word "evolution" is now applied to most natural changes or micro evolution, including cosmos. His 1859 book "On the Origin of Species" is still the current exemplar for common ancestors and his theory is presently taught by most educational institutes as a fact. Although there is no proof for macro evolution, his ideas were immediately accepted by humanists, secularists and atheists. Darwin studied at Cambridge to be an Anglican clergyman, but lost faith in God when his favorite daughter died. He had 10 children, but lost another two at childbirth. He called himself an agnostic and used Bible mainly for ethical guidance. He was horrified at the thought that his brains developed from monkey's brain. He was often sick and used "water treatment" for cure. He was the author of many books on nature, including "The Decent of Man and Selection in Relations to Sex" and "The Expression of the Emotions in Man and Animals". But he had no idea of human DNA and knew noting about molecular science. He thought that we consisted of protoplasm. His most rabid supporter was Thomas Henry Huxley, who referred to protoplasm as "The physical basis of life". Although rumored, there is no direct evidence that Darwin accepting God before he died. He was buried next to Sir John Herschel, a famous astronomer and chemist, not next to Sir Isaac Newton as rumored, in the Westminster Abby church in London.

The theory of evolution and natural selection with the survival of the fittest has been the most damaging and dangerous belief in human history. Natural selection applies to the same species and has nothing to do with speciation. Mutations are deleterious and only damage existing life. There is no proof for macro evolution, only unsupported hypothesis. The defenseless lamb would have never survived without a preordained plan. Evolution is based on countless accidental events and chance circumstances. It is nothing more than a hypothetical conjecture to lower the value of human life to the level of animals. The bright light at the conception is a definite sign that there is more than flesh and bones to human life. When the sperm fertilizes the egg it creates a new human life. The unborn baby's physical appearance and the personality were preordained at conception. Conceptions by In Vitro fertilization, or outside woman's uterus, should be banned. The fertility clinics, which destroy many unwanted fertilized female eggs, are slaughterhouses of human life. Although SCOTUS Roe vs. Wade and Doe vs. Dalton decisions made abortion legal in USA, it is the murder of live unborn babies, adopted from the barbaric pagan customs. If a woman is barren, she can adopt an unwanted baby and eliminate at least one planned abortion. Women claiming that an unborn baby is part of woman's body and they have a "choice" to keep it or abort it, are deciding between life and death of a human being. A fertilized egg is NOT PART OF WOMANS BODY! Although men play a part in the pregnancy, it is the women who are demanding the abortions. There would be no abortionists if women have the babies adopted and not aborted. The presumption that abortion is nothing more than discarding a fetus, has been the excuse for killing of billions of lives.

The history of holocausts by communism, Nazism, fascism and Jihad are all based on the evolutionary belief that human lives are not sanctified. The latest statistics reveal that there are about 40 million yearly voluntary abortion in the world, either chemically induced or performed by operation. Over 27 million, or most of the abortions, were performed in Africa. The excuse of controlling the world population by abortions is reprehensible. Adoption, not abortion and birth control before the woman's egg is fertilized are the only humane methods to stop the killing. Within 38 years (from 1973 to 2011) after Roe vs. Wade verdict there has been 53 million abortions in USA.

13 | Big Bang Controversy

Was Big Bang (BB) the birth of the universe? The reality is, universe does exists, either created by design or accident. Creation is the beginning or the original act of making, inventing or producing something new. This study examines the creation of the Universe from the Biblical manuscripts and then by the Big Bang theory in the Standard Model, including the latest discoveries. The English language translation of the six day Scriptural creation in Genesis 1 and 2 is based on the Masoratic texts.

Interpretation Of Biblical Creation

1. HISTORY

This study starts with the research of the origin of the Hebrew Bible. Abram (Abraham - *father of multitude)* (1996-1822 BCE) was the founder of Hebrew nation and the father of Isaac *(laughter)*, Ishmael *(whom God hears)* and six other children, including Midian *(strife)* with wife Keturah. He was born in Ur Kasdim (of the Chaldees), the present day Urfa in South East Turkey, north of Syrian border on the Plain of Shinar, which is about 80 kilometers from the Euphrates river. NOTE: Abraham was not born in the Sumerian City/State of Ur, which was located close to the mouth of the Euphrates river. This City of Ur was the largest city in the world at that time about thousands of miles from the City of Haran in Syria where Abraham stopped on the way to Canaan. There is no other City of Haran close to City/State Ur. When Abraham received the divine command by God to go to Canaan, the "promised land", he left Ur with his wife and half-sister Sarah *(princess)*, his nephew Lot *(veil)* and his father Terah *(station)* and went to the City of Haran. Haran is in Northern Syria, just South of Ur, in the beautiful valley below Mount Masius between the Euphrates and Khabour rivers. Abraham waited there until his father Terah, the idolater, died. Terah was the ancestor to Israelites, Ishmaelites,

Midianites, Moabites and Ammonites. The present name of Israel *(the prince that prevails with God)* was given to Jacob, GEN 32:28, the second son of Isaac, born 1837 BCE. It became the national name to all 12 tribes, and then as the Northern kingdom only, not including Judea.

The creation days in the Bible are recorded in GENESIS 1 & 2 with additional details in Psalms, Job, and in other Old Testament books. The first 5 books of Moses *(saved from the water)* (1571 -1451 BCE.), an Israelite, are called Pentateuch or Torah. God gave to Moses by "word of mouth" on Mount Sinai the laws, customs and traditions to be handed down and memorized from generations to generations. When Israelites arrived at Mount Sinai in Wilderness in 1489 BCE, God asked Moses to write down "all these words" in EX 17:14, 24:4 & 34:27, NU 33:2 and DEU 31:9. The writer of all books in Torah are credited to Moses, except his death, which was added by Ezra *(help)*. There are no original scripts of Moses' writing showing the alphabet he used to write the Pentateuch. Since Moses spent his first 40 years in Egyptian Pharaoh's court, he learned to write in 700 - 800 symbols of Hieroglyphs containing 24 uniliterals (single consonants) with biliteral and triliteral signs, which were never made into true alphabet. After discovering that he was an Hebrew, Moses must have also learned the original Proto-Sinaitic system, representing the language of all the Semitic-speaking workers in Egypt, including the Hebrew slaves. This Semitic Proto-alphabet, which is related to the older Egyptian Hieroglyphs, is now the basis of nearly all the present-day alphabet scripts. Moses spent the next 40 years in exile as an Egyptian tending the flock of Reuel, or Jethro the priest of Midians. Since Midianites, or the present day Arabians were the enemies of Israel, Moses was known to them as an Egyptian to avoid persecution. The Proto-Siniatic/Proto-Canaanite alphabet developed into Phoenician, which is a variant of the Paleo-Hebrew alphabet. The Paleo-Hebrew system was used until 5th Century BCE when it was replaced by Aramaic alphabet. The presently used alphabet in the Hebrew Bible has close relationship to the Imperial Aramaic script. Another branch of the Paleo-Hebrew alphabet is the Samaritan alphabet used in the writing of the Samaritan

Pentateuch. These alphabets contain 22 letters, all consonants, with 4 Matres lectonis, or sometime use as long vowels.

Ptolemy II (283-246 BCE), king of Egypt sponsored the translation of the five Books of Torah into Koine Greek by 70 Jewish scholars, which is now called the Septuagint. It is also known as the Old Greek Testament. The archaic Greece alphabet used the 22 symbols of the Phoenician alphabet until 400 BCE, when it was replaced with the 24-letter alphabet still used in Greece today. The translation of the Tanakh of the Hebrew Bible or the Old Testament protocanon was started in the 3rd Century BCE and completed in 1st Century BCE with 60% Masoratic interpretations. The oldest extant fragments of Genesis creation story is dated to 1st Century BCE. The paleographic Dead Sea Scrolls manuscripts, including fragments of all books in the Old Testament, except Esther, were dated from 225 BCE to 50 CE. The exegesis, or critical interpretation of the fragments, revealed 225 Biblical texts or nearly 22% of the total manuscripts of the OT written in Hebrew and Aramaic alphabets .

God prohibited the scribal editing of instructions received by Moses. Since no original scripts of his writings have been discovered, all the different editions of the Torah are not a deliberate violations of DEU 4:2 & 12:32. The Ten Commandments, written by God on the tablets of stone (EX 32:16), broken by Moses in EX 32:19 and rewritten by God in EX 34:28.

Talmud is now the central text of Rabbinic Judaism with the code for all Jewish laws given in parable by tractate. Talmud has 6200 pages with two constituent parts: "Mishnah" (200 CE) of the oral Torah and the "Gemara" (500 CE), or the analysis of Mishnah, edited by Rabbi Yehudah haNasi, and written in Aramaic. After the Talmudic period the Masorates (600-750 CE), or the Jewish scribes added vowel and grammatical guides in the margins of the Hebrew Bible. The fifth edition of the Masorah of Biblia Hebraica Stuttgartensia by the late Hans Peter Rüger is the continuation of the consummate work of Kittel. The Ben Hyyim (1524-5) Second Rabbinic Bible, also known as the Bomberg Bible or Texus Receptus was deleted from the Kittel's Hebrew Bible (1937), These marginal notes in the Masorah of Biblia

Hebraica Stuttgartensia are written in a form of abbreviated Aramaic using standard Tiberian pronunciations and graphic systems, representing the Leningrad Codex B19a. The 24 Masoratic texts, called Tanakh or Mikra, form the present Hebrew Bible (Biblia Hebraica). The Christian Old Testament has 39 Books by combining some of the 24 Books of the Hebrew Bible. Constatine the Great called 318 religious leaders to the First Council of Nicaea in 325 CE to form the canons of Christian doctrinal orthodoxy. The first English language Bible was the William Tyndale translation printed in 1525 CE. The King James of England Version of the Bible was completed in 1611 CE by 47 scholars from Church of England and is the basis of the present text for most Bibles.

2. BIBLICAL TEXT

NOTE: The English pronunciation of the Hebrew words are in *italics*.

GEN 1:1 "In the beginning God created *(baw-raw)* the heavens and the earth..."

GEN 1:2 "...and the earth being without form and empty, and darkness on the face of the deep, and the Spirit of God moving gently on the face of the waters".

GEN 1:5 "And there was evening *(ehreb from awrab)* and there was morning *(boker from bawkar)* day *(yome)* one *(ekhawd)"*.

GEN 1:16 "And God made *(awsaw - provided, accomplished)* the two great luminaries: the great luminary to rule a day and, and the small luminary and the stars to rule the night."

GEN 1:19 "And there was evening and there was morning the fourth day".

GEN 2:2 On the seventh day God rested from all His work. There was no "evening and morning" on the seventh day. The 7th day is definitely not a 24 hour Earth day.

3. ANALYSIS

There are three heavens. God is and always has been in the third heaven, DEU 10:14 & 1KINg 8:27. The mid-heaven or midst of the heavens is for angels, GEN 28:12, REV 8:13, 14:6 & 19:17. The heaven created in GEN 1:1 is the visible heaven, sky.

GEN 1:5 The day one started with "evening" or dusk and disorder and ended in the "morning" or dawn and order. Day one is often incorrectly translated as the "first day". There were no days before DAY ONE. A day in the Scriptures can be presently, seasonally, perpetually or just a certain day, as in "The Lords Day". God's day is not a twenty -four hour Earth day, or one rotation of the Earth. It is irrational to believe that God watched the rotation of the Earth when creating the "Heaven and Earth".

GEN 1:14 - 16 The luminaries, the sun and the moon, were created on Day One, but the light shown on Earth was only on the fourth day. No "evening" and "morning" until the Fourth Day on Earth.

GEN 2:2 There was no "evening and morning" on the seventh day. Even if God started His rest on the seventh day there has been no "morning", or end to the seventh day.

"God's Days" are the length of time before we measured time by the rotation of the Earth. The Day One is the beginning of time and the creation of the Universe. The Gospel according to

John 1:1 - 5 describes it: "In the beginning was the Word, and the Word was with God, and the Word was God. He (Jesus Christ) was in the beginning with God. All things came into being through Him, and without Him not even one thing came into being that has come into being. In Him was life, and the life was the light of men, and the light shines in the darkness, and the darkness did not overtake it". The details and the sequence of the conditions in the Universe after Big Bang are the same as these Biblical creation days. The Scriptural creation written by Moses was received from a direct communication with God. The Universe and life on Earth was not an accident, but was created by Christ, COL 1:16. "For all things were created for Him, the things in the Heavens and the things on the Earth; visible and invisible; whether thrones or lordships, or rulers, or authorities, all things have been created through Him and for Him".

Examining the Big Bang Cosmology

1. HISTORY OF STANDARD MODEL (SM)

All through history people have been questioning their existence. To this day many are worshiping the nature or believe in a secular humanistic god. Aristotle (384-322 BCE) was the first scientist in history whose Judeo-Islamic philosophical and theological thoughts carried into the Middle Ages and still influence the scholastic tradition of the Catholic Church. Aristotle was a pupil of Plato and believed that the Universe had infinite past. In 1927 the Belgian priest Georges Lemaitre (1984-1966 CE) proposed the Universe is expanding and had a beginning. Next step was the combining the electromagnetic and weak interaction forces by Sheldon Glashostrong discovery in 1961. In 1970 the Big Bang hypothesis was included in the Standard Model, after the discovery of fundamental particles interaction.

2. Big Bang Hypothesis with Latest Updates

The Universe emerged 13.8 billion of years ago from an explosion. The assumed age is based on Cosmic Microwave Background Radiation (CMBR). The origin of the explosion, or the Big Bang in the SM theory, was based on a subatomic particle or a quark. Then Stephen Hawking claimed that singularity of an infinitesimally small black hole was the cause. The present hypothesis is "One fundamental force caused the explosion". At the BB the temperature was so high that no particles existed. It is called the "Planck epoch". All the four Gauge bosons or force carriers were unified until one hundredth of million trillion trillion trillionth of a second (43 zeros) after the BB. As the Universe cooled the force of gravity separated from the other forces within a trillionth of trillion trillionth of a second after the BB. Then within the millionth of trillion trillionth of a second electromagnetism and weak interaction forces separated from the strong force. Then immediately after the BB explosion Universe experienced inflation, or faster than the speed of light expansion. The unknown duration of inflationary expansion of the Universe is a hypothesized field beyond our present-day physics. The assumption of Universe doubling 60 times or more within the first second after BB has no proof. Until the discovery of the Higgs boson (God's particle) , the Higgs field, dark matter and dark energy the SM early Universe cosmology scenario started with quark-gluon plasma. However, the hot plasma cosmology was rejected by most scientists in 2015 without replacing it with any other source for the particles. At a millionth of a second after the BB the hadrons were formed. Hadrons are composites of quarks or antiquarks. One second after the Big Bang most hadrons and antihadrons were eliminated by annihilation, leaving a small residue of hadrons for the visible Universe. Between one and three seconds after Big Bang the Universe was dominated by leptons/antileptons. There are 6 types of leptons or elementary particles like electrons. For every lepton matter particle there was a corresponding lepton antimatter particle and after the annihilation only a small residue of leptons remained. The matter/antimatter annihilations created photons to visible universe. Photons dominated the Universe until three seconds after the Big Bang. Between three and twenty minutes after the Big Bang protons and neutrons formed the atomic nuclei. For every billion mutual annihilations a particle of matter remained and the existing matter in the Universe are the left-over particles after the annihilation with antimatter. The explanation for this phenomena is called "charge-parity" (CP) symmetry violation. After Higgs boson discovery and the extension of Higgs Field to quantum field that permeates all space, it is now the latest explanation where Gauge bosons obtained the mass.

3. ANALYSIS

The postulated age of the 13.8 billion year old expanding Universe is based on the red-shifted photons measurements of Cosmic Microwave Background Radiation (CMBR). According to the SM theory radiation started 378,000 years after the Big Bang (BB), when electrons and protons recombined into hydrogen atoms. The paradox is, the estimated age of the star HD140283 in the Milky Way galaxy, nicknamed "Methuselah", is 14.46 billion years, or over half a billion years older than the Universe! The star is only 190 light years from Earth and NASA's Hubble Space Telescope was able to measure a precise parallax. Also, the 7.085 red-shift of the ULASJ1120+0641 quasar comoving distance of approx. 29 billion light years happened almost 14 billion years before the BB. This is a clear proof that there is no connection between distances from the Earth and the age of the star and the universe. Without knowing the location of the BB explosion in the Universe, all estimated ages are nothing more than postulates. Einstein predicted the effects of gravitational waves in the 1916 theory of General relativity as "Ripples or curvature in the spacetime". Based on the Andre Linde feigned theory of inflation, the expansion of the Universe in less than a trillionth second, should be observable on Earth as the mythical gravitational wave. Cosmologists were hoping to detect B-modes (magnetic) polarization of the CMBR, or the hypothetical gravitational waves in the early Universe, using upgraded BICEP 3 (Background Imaging of Cosmic Extragalatic Polarization) instruments at South Pole. However, the BICEP 2 claim of gravitational wave detection was discarded on June 18, 2014 and to this date no definite location for the BB has been detected. CMBR research also revealed that the Universe is homogenous with no hotter regions. This means, the observable Universe has no center and no single point for the BB explosion. An uncontrolled BB explosion would result in isotropic Universe and expand in all directions simultaneously. But our observable Universe is almost a flat anisotropic disc with 28 billion parsecs or 93 billion light years diameter. NOTE: One parsec is 3.26156 light years. We have no idea what is beyond the observable Universe. Is it infinite and filled with endless galaxies or is it empty space? We have no conception of infinity or the size of the cosmos. We can only observe Universe as far as the end of 46.5 billion light year radius from Earth. When dividing this radius with the hypothetical 13.8 light year age of the BB, the size of the observable Universe has 3.37 times (46.5 : 13.8) larger expansion than possible with the maximum speed of light expansion. Light travels 186,000 miles per second and one light year is 5.88 trillion miles. According to SM, the diameter of the observable Universe is 93 billion light years and when multiplying it with 5.88 trillion miles per year, the diameter of the Universe is 547 billion trillion miles (21 zeros).

Cosmic inflation is Alan Guth's unproven hypothesis of nascent Universe passing through "Positive vacuum energy". Although it is now part of the Quantum Field Theory, it is the <u>worst</u>

theoretical prediction in the history of physics called VACUUM CATASTROPHE. Empty space in the observable Universe is NOT A VACUUM. The WMAP satellite launched in 2001 and the Planck 2009 satellite proved the HUBBLE constant has no relationship to the age of the Universe. Cosmologists have accepted the presence of Dark Matter, Dark Energy, Antimatter and Higgs Field being everywhere in the Universe, without actually being able to detect them.

In addition to the above unproven and missing evidences , BB has many other problems; "A Cupsy Halo" problem, "A Dwarf Galaxy" problem, "Magnetic Monopoles" problem, "Baryogenesis speculative hypothesis" , "Black Hole singularity", "Horizon Problem" (or the same temperature but greater distances) and the source of the original Fundamental Force, the appearance of Hot Plasma and the energy/force required to form over hundred billion trillion stars with planets, interstellar and intergalatic media into perfect sheets and filaments in the observable Universe.

4. CONCLUSION

To compare the true evidence of creation vs. BB evolutionary Universe, it is necessary to eliminate all postulates and hypothesis based on unproven theories. Scriptural creation Days were written by Moses at the direction of God. Unless there is proof that Moses did not exist or did not obey God's instructions for writing the Torah, we must accept it at faith.

The evolutionary hypothesis of the BB is based on postulates with many unproven and missing evidences. Cosmologists continually "update" the "scientific" hypothesis about the mysterious Universe. Hopefully, some of the problems connected with BB hypothesis will be solved with the new hyper-physics. Even, if we discover more and more what God has created, there is much we will never know. We have no conception of infinity, the inherent information contained in the particles and the cause for the beginning. Also, there are no rational answers to the inexplicable amount force/energy contained in the observable and the invisible Universe. The birth of the Universe and the beginning of time is possible only with God's creation. God is the foremost scientist of the world.

Cosmologists have discovered only a fraction what God has created. To call God's creation "unscientific" only reveals their ignorance. If BB was nothing more than an accident then it must be a MIRACLE. It is your choice, either believe in God or in miracles.

14

Where Was the Garden of Eden?

This research starts with the biblical description of the Garden of Eden. To verify the location of the Garden of Eden it is paramount to determine when God planted it. One method to determine the age of it is to establish the age of Adam, the first human to occupy it. This study also compares the age of the first human species on earth published in the most recent scientific reports of geneticists, archaeologists, genealogists, climatologists, geologists, hydrologists, paleontologists and paleoanthropologists. The Scriptures are quoted from 1611 King James Bible version and translation from root words in Strong's Concordance*. Whether you are atheist or Christian this research will provide new insight to a better understanding of the history of human origin.

When Was Garden of Eden Created

The description of the Garden of Eden in GEN 2:8 is "And the Lord God planted a garden eastward in Eden; and there He put the man (adam*) whom He had formed (yatsar*)". The man was created in GEN 1:26 " And God said, Let Us make (asah*) man in Our image, after Our likeness..." The "Us" refers to a trinity of God, God's Son Jesus and the Holy Spirit. In GEN 2:7 God describes how the first man was created: "And the LORD God formed(yatsar*) man of the dust of the ground, and breathed into his nostrils the breath of life; and man became living soul". In GEN 2:18 "And the LORD God said, it is not good that the man should be alone; I will make him an help meet for him". But no animal helper suited him. In GEN 2:21-24 God formed a Woman and in GEN 3:20 the man called her Eve.

There are many studies and reports on the location of the Garden of Eden. This research starts by estimating the age of Garden of Eden from the genealogists analysis of human DNA. Since the ages of Adam and Eve are also the age of the Garden of Eden, the analyses of the rate of DNA mutations of the protein-coated gene changes in the human DNA should end with the first human. The secular geneticists research of the female 'X' Chromosomes in 1980's was named "Mitochondrial Eve". Their study of the 37 gene maternal mtDNA postulated: Eve lived in East Africa between 150,000 to 200,000 years ago. The biblical location for the Garden of Eden was Mesopotamia, but Adam and Eve were expelled from the Garden of Eden. So, East Africa location was a good possibility, as shown later in this study. The geneticists report was based on the assumption of one DNA mutation every 1000 years. Conveniently, this assumed rate corresponded with the archaeologists discovery of the 195,000 year old "Omo Remains" fossils in East Africa. Paleoanthrapologists claim that these are the first modern human fossils (Homo sapiens sapiens), but this was made without any conclusive support from DNA tests. All tests of the damaged ancient DNA, obtained from fossils, have been incomplete and the results have shown no relationship to human genome. The most recent research, however, revised the mtDNA mutation rate to 18 times higher what was used for the original Mitochondrial Eve study. This revelation completely invalidated the 1980's report changing the first woman's age to between 11,500 to 12,000 years ago. Another study of the 200 nuclear genes of male "y" Chromosomes called "y-Chromosomal Adam" was based on the rate of one mutation every 125 years. Again, there is no proof for this mutation rate. Also, the SRY (sex-determining region of y-Chromosomes protein), nor the cause and the original meiosis (cell division) to 59 million basic pairs is still unknown. Any claim for determining the age of the first man, based on archaeology, is not supported by any maxims.

Contrary to paleoanthropologists claim that some of the bipedal primates are modern human ancestors, there is no conclusive proof for it. Homo habilis, Homo erectus, Homo sapiens, Neanderthal man, etc. are all animals. The analysis of all ancient DNA sequences have been outside the modern human mtDNA variation. Animals have at least 4% different genome from the present day humans, but most geneticists ignore this fact and promote only evolution. Even an infinitesimally small change in the 3 billion bases of DNA will create a totally different species. To include humans into animal ancestry, geneticists added one more "sapiens" to the animal "Homo sapiens" and called it "Homo sapiens sapiens" or modern human. This was a deliberate plan delude everybody and to promote their evolutionary belief for human existence. Also, to rely on the molecular clock for estimating the age is unreliable and can be biased towards substantial overestimation of time. To validate their belief in evolution, scientific "discoveries" are nothing more than postulates to fit their preconceived hypothesis.

Many Bible translators use 4,004 B.C. as the date for the creation of Adam. This means that in 2016 A.D. Adam would be 6020 (4,004 + 2016) years old. Close study of Adam's genealogy, however, reveals many gaps in the Bible genealogies. The word son *(huidos*)* was used not only for immediate off-springs, but also for remote kinship. As an example in Matthew 1:1 "The book of the generation of Jesus Christ, the son of David, the son of Abraham", the meaning of the word son was kinship. Jesus was not a son of David or son of Abraham. Yes, Jesus was in David's ancestry through Mary, but God was the father of Jesus Christ.

The Earth has suffered more than 5 major ice ages. The last ice age from 120,000 - 12,000 years ago peaked about 20,000 years ago. Ice covered Northern Europe, Russia and Canada, including many Northern States in America. The sea levels were over 120 meters or up to 475 feet below the present water levels. There was no Persian Gulf until after the ice melted. The deepest water depth in the Persian Gulf is now 90 meters or 295 feet, but during the ice age it was a dry land and the bottom of the Gulf was more than 180 feet (475 ft - 295 ft) above the sea level. There was a dry land connection between Persia (Iran) and the Arabian peninsula. Also, when the Gulf of Aden water levels were 475 feet lower than now, there was a dry land connection between to Yemen from the present administrative Bari region of Somalia at the Horn of Africa. The large islands of Socotra, Sambah and high ridges under the Gulf of Aden provided direct land connection between Africa and Asia. The research for first human ended with Mitochondrial Eve in East Africa. Since Adam and Eve were expelled from the Garden of Eden, it is quite probable that they moved to East Africa. Since Archaeologists have discovered lots of ancient bipedal primates fossils in East Africa, it was the cradle of many life forms.

At the end of the ice age the earth experienced abrupt climate changes called Oldest Dryas, Older Dryas and Younger Dryas. For short periods between 12,000 - 11,800 BCE radiocarbon years the average temperature increased up to 18°F in Mesopotamia. The warm climate melted the ice and supplied water to the four rivers of the Garden of Eden. It produced lush vegetation and forests in Mesopotamia. Also, the monsoon rains, starting 10,500 years ago in North Africa, turned the Sahara Desert into fertile environment. To establish the approximate age of the Garden of Eden the most important factor was the Older Dryas rapid climate change and the melting of the ice after the ice age. This corresponds with the post-Pleistocene period of the present day Holocene epoch, which began 11,700 years ago.

Where Was the Garden of Eden?

The first five books in the Bible, called The Pentateuch or Torah by the Jews, were written by Moses, born in Goshen, Egypt in 1571 B.C. The death of Moses, described in the book of Deuteronomy was added by Ezra. It was Ezra, the famous scribe and priest, who settled the Old Testament Canon of Scriptures after the return from Babylon. Moses was the greatest prophet in the Old Testament. In Exodus he had many direct communications with the Lord and spoke to Jehovah "mouth to mouth" (NUM: 12-8). God made especial revelations only to Moses by personally giving him the law on Mount Sinai. There are three Song of Moses, the last one in Deuteronomy, written to Israelites before his death in 1451 B.C. It was for prophetic and didactic purposes. Some Earlier documents in Cuneiform describing the Garden of Eden also supported GEN 2:10-14 version written by Moses. The names of the rivers and the description of land in Genesis apply mostly to 15-th century B.C. usage. "And a river went out of Eden to water the garden, and from there it was parted and became four heads. The name of the first is Pison: that it is which compass-eth the whole land of Havilah, where there is gold; and the gold of that land is good; there is bdellium and the onyx stone. And the name of the second river is Gihon - the same is it that compasseth the whole land of Ethiopia. And the name of the third river is Hidekel: that is it which goeth toward east of Assyria. And the fourth river is Euphrates."

Moses did not start naming the sources of the four rivers. First he described the river out of Garden of Eden, which flowed towards the mouth of the river. He did not name this river or where the mouth of the river was. The first river Pison is in the land of Havilah, located in South-West part of Arabian peninsula. There are still many abandoned gold mines and onyx visible on the land. Havilah had many trees after the ice age suitable for obtaining bdellium gum raisin. Although there is no present Pison river, there is a 600 kilometer dry river valley south of Medina called Wadi el Batin and 425 kilometer dry valley called Wadi al Rummah to Kuwait border.

The second river Gihon was surrounding the present day Ethiopia. It is also called the land of Cush. Cush was the grandson of Noah and the father of Nimrod. His kindred lived on both sides of the Red Sea from South Arabian peninsula all the way to Euphrates river in Mesopotamia. Bagrawiyah was the capital of the Kingdom of Cush (or Kush). It was located on the east side of the Nile river. There are pyramids of the Kushite rulers at Meroe, where the Blue Nile and White Nile rivers merge at the present day city of Khartoum, Sudan. The Ethiopian Highlands Batu mountain Lake Tana is the present source of the Blue Nile river and was the probable source for the Gihon river. During the ice age when the sea levels were 475 feet lower than now, there was a solid land connection between the Horn of Africa and the Arabian peninsula. Socotra, the largest island and several smaller islands, like Sambah, formed a land bridge with underwater ridges of the Gulf of Aden from Ethiopia to Yemen. Earthquakes and volcanic activity in East Africa, Arabian peninsula and Mesopotamia have altered the topography of lands and the depth of the seas since the planting of the Garden of Eden. The Earth crust's longest and deepest known earthquake fault is 5000 kilometers long starting in Lebanon, then south through Dead Sea, Red Sea and ending in Mozambique, Africa. The most likely source for the Gihon river was the Tana Lake in Ethiopia flowing over the land bridge between Africa and Asia from the Horn of Africa to Arabian peninsula and then to Mesopotamia.

The third river Hidekel is the present day Tigris. Ancient Assyria encompassed most of the Northern Mesopotamia, Syria and ended in Turkey. In the center of Assyria was the city of Nineveh, founded by Nimrod the son of Cush, located on the East bank of Tigris. The present day city of Mosul in Iraq is on the West bank of the Tigris river, opposite to the ancient Nineveh.

There is no reference for the location of the fourth river Euphrates. In GEN 16:18 and other Scriptures Jehovah gave the land to Abram seed, from the river of Egypt and from Lebanon to the great river of Euphrates, or the present day Israelites.

Water on the surface of the Earth always flows to

the lowest point. During the ice age, the Persian Gulf was dry land with the lowest point at the Strait of Hormuz, the mouth of the river out of the Garden of Eden. The course of the river out of the Garden of Eden is the present day Strait of Hormuz between the Persian Gulf and the Gulf Oman. Even now the remains of the ice age Glacier-carved coasts of polar region are still visible in Strait of Hormuz.

Conclusion

Based on the description in GEN 2:10-14 Garden of Eden was located north of present day United Arab Emirates, within 60 miles from Abu Dhabi and 30 miles from Dubai. It was planted by God 12,000 years ago, but Garden of Eden is now at the bottom of Persian Gulf.

15 | Compendium

This book describes theories, postulates and hypothesis on cosmos and human life on earth, including the latest discoveries in 2016. The author of this book also offers original theories and conclusions to provide answers to many questions not available in SM or determined by the scientific method. Some of the conclusions are controversial and contradict presently accepted theories and hypothesis, but they are more logical and provable than the commonly accepted "scientific" principles, which are based on assumptions, postulates, hidden variables and conjectures.

The original theories are the "Realistic Theory of Galaxies" and "Where was the Garden of

Eden?" The "Big Bang Controversy" chapter discloses what alphabet God used to write the TEN COMMANDMENTS and what language Moses used to communicate with the Hebrew slaves. It also proves that "Big Bang" and "Inflation" are not feasible under the present day physics. It denies the existence of "Dark matter" & "Primordial Hot Plasma", and disputes "Quantum Field Theories"of "Quantum Tunnelling", "Quantum Chromodynamics"& "Quantum Electrodynamics", "Primordial Nucleosynthesis", "Baryogenesis", "Cosmological, Hubble and Gravitational Constants", "Supersymmetry", "M-Theories", "De Broglie Waves", "Meiosis", "Black Holes Cold Dark Matter" and so more.

Scientific method has never established the existence of the mysterious "Dark or Vacuum Energy" or the "Fundamental Force". Scientists are still searching for the elusive "Graviton particles" and the subatomic particle Neutrino mass. There is no proof for the "Wave/particle Duality", "Electric Dipole Moment" or the "Magnetic Monopoles". Also, cosmologists have never solved the "EPR Paradox" or "Quantum Entanglement", "Vacuum Catastrophe" and the "Black Hole Horizon Problems". They are keeping eerie silence about the incalculable amount of energy, in the form of visible and invisible matter, in the universe. This was the energy which gave birth to the primordial universe. It was not an accidental Big Bang, it was God's preordained plan for cosmos. Either you believe in miracles or in God's design and creation of life on earth.

Maps of the Garden of Eden

CPSIA information can be obtained
at www.ICGtesting.com
Printed in the USA
BVOW06s1510011116

466543BV00013B/64/P